eat your heart out

eat your heart out

The Look Good, Feel Good, Silver Lining Cookbook

DEAN SHEREMET

The Countryman Press

A divison of W. W. Norton & Company

Independent Publishers Since 1923

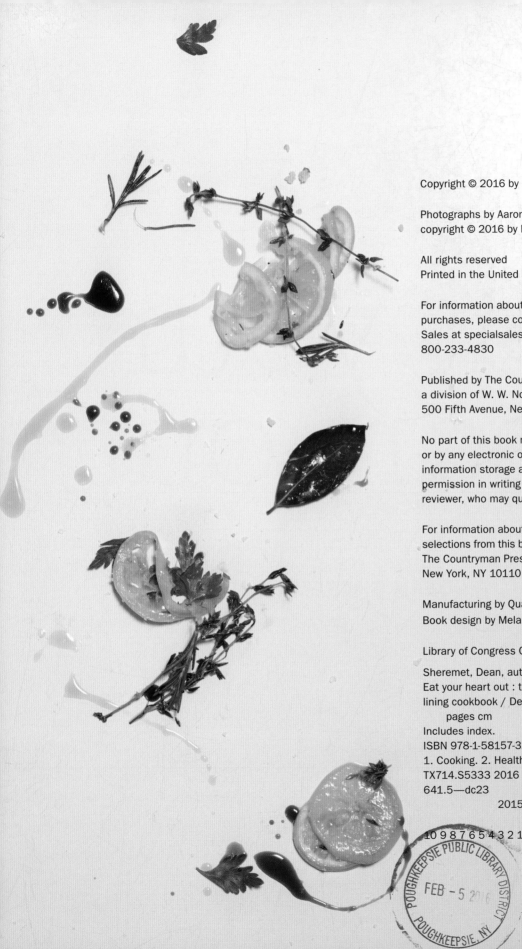

For information about special discounts for bulk
purchases, please contact W. W. Norton Special
Sales at specialsales@wwnorton.com or
800-233-4830

Published by The Countryman Press,
a division of W. W. Norton & Company, Inc.,
500 Fifth Avenue, New York, NY 10110

Manufacturing by QuadGraphics Taunton
Book design by Melanie Ryan

Library of Congress Cataloging-in-Publication Data

Sheremet, Dean, author.
Eat your heart out : the look good, feel good, silver
lining cookbook / Dean Sheremet.
     pages cm
Includes index.
ISBN 978-1-58157-329-9 (hardcover)
1. Cooking. 2. Health. I. Title.
TX714.S5333 2016
641.5—dc23
     2015034171

10 9 8 7 6 5 4 3 2 1

To the three most important women in my life:

My grandmother, Stella, who instilled tough love and old-school virtues in me from a young age.

To my Mother, for always understanding me, supporting me, and giving me the freedom to be who I am.

To my lovely and talented wife, Sarah—I couldn't have written this book without you. You've seen me through every step of my culinary and emotional journey.
You are my constant source of inspiration.

Contents

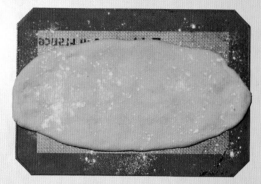

Acknowledgments:

The most important lesson I learned after completing this cookbook had very little to do with food. I was reminded of how many incredible and loving friends I am surrounded by who always come to the table for me in times of need. Everyone's collaborations, from pre-production to during the shoot, helped me fully realize and achieve this dream of a project.

AARON CAMERON MUNTZ—We finally did it! I always knew you would shoot beautiful images for this book, but the results ended up even more beautiful than I could have ever imagined.

MEG THOMPSON—Not only are you the most beautiful book agent in the world, but you are also the most honest and true. Thank you for constantly talking me off the ledge when I got discouraged and thank you for never backing down.

LAUREN KUCERAK—You are the ultimate connector and you've never doubted me for a minute. Thank you for being a friend and incredible motivator.

MARÍA DEL MAR CUADRA—You are my culinary better half and the images came to life through your brilliant art direction and minimalist styling.

ANN TREISTMAN and the whole team at Norton/Countryman for taking a chance and believing in my message, and letting the food speak for itself.

COTY TARR—My brotha from anotha motha, thank you for always making me look good and always stepping up and killing it when I call. Also—can I get a little more Uncle Phil in there?

MELANIE RYAN—You were so gracious to help me make a beautiful proposal and now an absolutely beautiful book.

FRANKLIN THOMPSON—Your infectious laugh kept me going on these extremely long and challenging days. Thanks for helping to keep us on track and backing us up on the technical side.

MAYA ROSSI—Thank you for finding a way to execute my champagne dreams on a beer budget. You were a great sport in dealing with my crazy antics on set. Always remember to "be better."

ROBERT KIDD—Thanks for lending your expertise and keeping me entertained with your stories.

DAVID WHITE—Thank you for opening your home to us and always providing an environment for me to be creative in.

Introduction:
Love, Loss, and
How the Kitchen Saved Me

She cheated, I got dumped, and we divorced. I'd like to say it was conscious uncoupling, but the truth is, I got knocked on my ass.

That's the CliffsNotes version of the demise of my marriage to LeAnn Rimes. When we split up, the press had so many questions, and I avoided answering them. All I wanted anyone to know back then was the condensed version—we tried, she hurt me, we failed—which means that there is so much of that story that went untold, so many more discoveries made that I kept to myself, until now.

When my marriage ended, so did the fairy tale, and I had to finally wake up and face my fate. I wished my ego had let me see the ending sooner, because it was over long before I ever realized it. I wanted to blame her, I wanted to blame him, but for the first time in my life, I realized that the blame fell squarely on my shoulders. I had been the one who was foolish enough to get caught up in a lifestyle that was so different from my own upbringing, a world where Ferraris, Porsches, and private planes were the norm, where dinner parties were populated with more stars than the Billboard 100.

But how could a 20-year-old from a middle-class family in Detroit *not* have been enticed by that?

Now that time has passed, I'm ready to answer all the questions the reporters kept throwing at me—about what happened to break me, and more important, what I did to heal.

My heart was broken and my life was in pieces. Cooking helped me put myself back together again, recipe by recipe, dish by dish, and meal by meal.

ONCE UPON A TIME . . .

My life with LeAnn wasn't always filled with craziness. While we were living in Nashville, we were anyone's definition of a normal young couple. I loved her more than I had ever loved anything. That period felt so normal and grounded.

On a professional level, LeAnn and I worked incredibly well together. We collaborated on everything from music videos to live performances, and I was getting my writing itch scratched as well. I was engaging in all of the creative possibilities offered by my role in her organization, and for a while, I was happy. When I wasn't writing or choreographing, I was throwing the most amazing dinner parties, with guest lists that read like the Billboard HOT 100, and I was cooking all of the food! I loved it.

LeAnn had the spotlight in our relationship, and at that time, I embraced it. I felt that rather than live separate lives chasing a similar dream, I would funnel all of my creative energy into her career. As a professional dancer, I knew what it took to keep one's body running at an athlete's level, so I got LeAnn into the gym and insisted that I cook most of our meals, especially on the road. I knew how to get results, and instead of focusing on helping myself, it was all about her.

When we love people, we want to make things perfect for them—sometimes at the expense of ourselves. I'm a passionate and obsessive person, and I have an insane work ethic. It's why I've been able to be successful onstage and in the kitchen. I became obsessed with helping LeAnn's career, constantly wanting to make things better for her. Even to the point of insanity.

I loved her more than I loved myself, and that's where I went wrong. It was all-consuming, and I could never shut it off. Over dinner, vacations, or just driving in the car, I would make suggestions about what we could do to make everything bigger and better. I wrote nonstop, choreographed nonstop, and constantly came up with strategies to get her back on top. That drove her mad, and I realize now the part it may have played in our downfall. But the crazy thing is . . . it actually worked. She was fit as a fiddle, back on radio, and back in front of the country audience that she had previously abandoned.

It was a double-edged sword. Everything I viewed as a success continued to drive a bigger wedge between us, and she felt trapped. And whenever she felt cornered, she'd completely shut down.

LeAnn had spent her whole life being told what to do, how to stand, and how to act. I was the only one she *didn't* want to hear it from. That's the biggest lesson I learned: Sometimes space is the best thing. You can't protect the ones you love from everything. Sometimes you just need to walk away and let them breathe.

The more I put into her career, the less I felt that the relationship was reciprocal. Something was still missing. I felt I was wearing so many hats: father figure, husband, manager, and lover—probably in that order—and none of them ever seemed to fit properly. It was all about her, all the time, with no room for my needs and my hopes. Her success—the success that we were building together—left no room for me to grow as a human being.

The life—the dream life under the bright lights, with the big shows, with the thousands of screaming fans who had no idea what our lives were like after the applause died down and the lights went out—was completely unsustainable. The animosity built up within both of us. Thus began the heartbreaking downward spiral.

THE END

The day I finally did walk out the door, it was anything but liberating. It seemed like a strong, bold move, but it was really just another bluff to see whether I could stir some kind of emotion inside her to make her stay. We fought, we cried, and eventually I forced myself out the door for fear that I would cave.

My marriage was over, and I was destroyed. When LeAnn and I broke up, it shone a fluorescent light on the fact that I had put my life and my dreams on hold for almost a decade in support of someone else's career. We've all done that—given ourselves up to the needs of others and not saved enough for us.

Almost a decade of my life was gone. I realized that none of my hard work would ever really matter; I was a footnote in someone else's history. I had never known when to walk away, and eventually, I paid the ultimate price.

The worst part was that I did it to myself. No one

held a gun to my head; no one ever forced my hand. I had lived a life that was too comfortable, too safe, and *way* too secure. I hadn't gotten my hands dirty in a long time, and I had forgotten what it felt like to create something that was solely mine, that no one could ever take from me. I had forgotten how to make my own decisions. I'd forgotten how to be a man. I was nothing more than an accessory to someone else's life.

I had been living someone else's dream.

THE BEGINNING

I got on the first plane headed for Nashville to stay with close friends. I couldn't go back to that giant empty house and be surrounded by all the lies that had become my truth. While I was staying with my friends, I had a lot of support, and a lot of time to think. I decided I had to be the master of my own fate. It was time to put my life on a completely different track—to get back on *my* track. I have always been infatuated with food, and had always threatened that one day I would go to culinary school. That is, whenever it might fit into LeAnn's schedule, or maybe if she ever did Broadway.

Now was my chance.

I spent three months back home with my mom and sisters to regroup, and it was sorely needed. When you make a break from something, you need to nurture yourself, and be nurtured by others. Family is everything to me. For a long time, I was always the one to give my family members advice; I was the one who made the brave step to move away from our small town and make them proud. For the first time I realized how much I had neglected them and how much I needed them.

I was a grown man, and I had to admit it: I needed my mother. If it weren't for her, I know I wouldn't have been able to survive the lowest lows. My parents got divorced when I was two, and my father took us to live with my grandmother. They simply didn't have the resources to raise me in the way they knew I should be brought up, and this was a heavy emotional burden my mom carried. She felt sad that she missed out on all of those years of togetherness, but in my mind, she more than made up for everything by being there for me when I returned home.

The wisdom she had gleaned during her divorce

from my father 30 years prior would come back to be some of the most valuable and cathartic lessons for us both, something I had never imagined. My return home taught me an important lesson: You just never know when or how the people you care about can teach you and help you as you grow and change. We sat together, we cooked together, we ate together, and we talked—and both of us got rid of the family ghosts that had been haunting us for so long.

I've had wonderful and expensive therapy, and it was all very helpful, but the best advice I ever got came from my mother: "Get it out of your system, get off your ass, and move on." *That* was the splash of ice-cold water that I needed thrown in my face.

REBIRTH

I remember moving into my *own* apartment after LeAnn and I separated as though it was yesterday. I felt as if my parents had just dropped me off at college for the first time. I could do whatever I wanted whenever I wanted! That was a feeling I never had in my past life. I was constantly scheduled to the minute every second of every day, on a plane, on a bus, or on a stage. When I got my own space, I finally had a quiet sanctuary that was mine and mine alone.

And I had my *own* kitchen, which I set up to make all the food that I loved to eat. Finally, it wasn't about anyone else's preferences but my own. I was at a pivotal and transitional time, so I did the one thing I knew would make me feel better: I started cooking for myself.

I learned how to cook from my grandmother at a very young age. I probably cracked my first egg at three and made my first cake by six. Never did I imagine that wonderful time spent with her would lay the groundwork for the rest of my life. We didn't have a lot of money when I was growing up, and my mother wasn't in a place where she could take care of me. Enter my grandmother, who came out of retirement to raise me and bankroll my dance lessons. To this day, I know that without her influence, things probably would have turned out far differently than they have for me. She was a rigid yet loving woman who instilled a fierce work ethic in me that I hold dear to this day. Most important, she taught me how to feed myself, which is the foundation of self-care.

Her wisdom, and the kitchen skills she showed

me as a boy, have carried me through all the ups and downs life threw at me when I became a man.

For me, the kitchen was my rebirth by fire. All of the energy I had spent on someone else—helping LeAnn get fed, helping LeAnn get fit—was for me now, and I was determined to spend it wisely.

Getting "it" out of your system is only possible when you accept that change is inevitable and embrace self-care. I asked others for help when I needed it, and I got it, but ultimately I had to help myself. I already knew how to cook, but I wanted to be an even better chef, and I was ready for a new point of view.

So, shortly after I moved into my new, smaller-than-before home but so much better because it was mine, I started my training at the French Culinary Institute (FCI). I was the biggest dork ever, and I absolutely loved it. I was much older than most of my classmates, and I took it very seriously. I was consumed with being the best. I volunteered for any and every big chef that came through our school for demos. I would go to class for eight hours during the day, and then I would assist Jacques Pépin, Jacques Torres, Paul Liebrandt, and Alfred Portale, to name a few, well into the night. I was never too proud to get my hands dirty. I hadn't felt that exhausted, respected, and fulfilled in a long time. I was on my way to happiness.

After I graduated top of my class from FCI, I started working at Nobu on 57th Street. All of my culinary school glory quickly faded as I was thrown into a *real* kitchen. No more four people on one station each taking turns to cook something. Every day I was expected to do the work of four people, and I got my ass kicked. "C'mon, *papi*, move your ass and don't cry" was something I heard often from my weathered station partner, German. He had been doing this since I was in grade school and had more energy than guys half his age. He never stopped moving, and neither did I. The constant chiding from your fellow cooks leads to one of two things: You get it, or you wash out. I got cut, cut down a size, and burned in the early days, but I was no stranger to adapting, and I quickly learned the system and eventually worked every station on my way up the ranks at Nobu.

But I wanted more. If I was going to do this, I wanted to go all the way. I wanted Michelin-starred fine dining, and that to me meant Jean-Georges. I was fortunate to know Johnny Iuzzini from years back, and he got me a meeting with the chef. It was like being brand new all over again . . . the lowest on the totem pole. The first few months cooking in Jean-Georges' sister restaurant Nougatine were a brutal far cry from the tall hats and grace that was happening upstairs. We were in the basement, and it was like *Thunderdome*: "Two men enter, one man leaves." It was either you or the guy next to you who was going upstairs first. I was the best in my previous kitchen, but I knew that here in this world of fine dining, *everyone* was the best in his or her previous kitchen, and I would have to give all I had to battle for my spot. And I would have to put myself first. I used to feel that I always had to announce my success or progress to the world, but in the kitchen, you put your head down, shut your mouth, and do your job. People notice when you lead by example and not ego. When I got the tall white hat and went upstairs to the main dining room, it was one of the happiest, most gratifying moments of my life.

Who knew a paper hat that cost about a dollar would become one of my most prized possessions? I had accomplished what I set out to do. I had finally arrived.

In my first New York apartment I used to have a dream board smack in the middle of my living room. It was something I looked at a hundred times a day. It was always there, and I couldn't ignore it. The top had a three-by-five card that I had handwritten that said, "Do your job." Then it said, "The rest will take care of itself."

My job was more than showing up to work every day; it was all the steps it took to be able to tackle the grand dreams that I had. First thing every morning, I had an energizing breakfast smoothie. I made many variations, but one of my favorites was usually comprised of almond milk, almond butter, a banana, two dates, and a pinch of cinnamon, and most important—a shot of espresso. Then I would hit the gym, run, or ride my bike to clear my head and prepare myself for the day ahead.

It was all about me.

The word *selfish* gets a bad rap, and it shouldn't. To fully love yourself, you need to shut out all the distractions and concentrate on healing. That all starts with putting the highest-quality food in your body and regularly breaking a sweat doing something fun. The first thing I tell anyone going through a divorce or a great loss is to look in the mirror. That's the person you need to take care of! When it's time to make a big change and do something that you never imagined you would do, you can only change your scenery, change your environment, and change your point of view—if you believe in yourself—and show yourself that you're worth it.

Part One:
Nurture Yourself

Chapter 1

To Begin Again:
Perfect Your Pantry

I want to share a secret about my past addiction . . . to kitchen tools and appliances. If there were actually a group called Williams-Sonoma Anonymous, I would have been the guy who ran all the meetings. I had every piece of gear imaginable: bread maker, avocado slicer, Slap Chop, onion dicer, and egg slicer. You name it, I had it, and it was fun when I had a giant pantry to tuck it all away in. As time went on and I became a serious cook, I realized I never used any of these silly things and, instead of saving me time, they just took up space and stressed me out to look at them.

If you live in a world where time, space, and money are no object, you can probably stop reading my book at this point. But all of my other *real* friends, listen up! You don't need that damn avocado slicer, and if I come over to your house and find it, I will throw it in the trash just after I berate you for having it.

In every kitchen I've ever been in, even in the finest restaurants and the biggest homes, space is at a premium. When it's at an extra premium, you have to be creative and resourceful with what's been given to you. I always tell people, "I'm in the make-it-happen business." There is no time to wait for the perfect tool; you sometimes have to create it. I've used a salt shaker and a coffee cup in lieu of a mortar and pestle, random sauté pans as pot lids that never seemed to be around when I needed them, and I've fashioned resealable plastic bags into pastry bags for cupcake piping. As one of my first chef's used to say, "If you don't have it, you don't need it."

Perfecting your pantry is about assembling the tools that *you* need to make the food that *you* love.

There are a lot of tools, I think, that are essential in your kitchen arsenal. In this chapter I include kitchen tools you need, kitchen tools you never need, the emotional and practical value of decluttering and organizing, and foods and spices to keep on hand for quick food prep.

KITCHEN TOOLS

Sauté pans should be of the sturdiest material you can afford. You don't need to have a whole set; start with an 8-inch and an iron skillet and you can make almost anything.

For Cooking and Baking

Small sauté pan: 8-inch

Medium-size sauté pan: 10-inch

Large sauté pan: 12-inch

Heavy cast-iron skillet: 8- to 10-inch

Nonstick skillet: 8-inch

Small saucepan: less than 2-quart, about 4 inches tall

Medium-size saucepan: about 2-quart, about 4 inches tall

Dutch oven: Does multiple duty; most soup, stew, and chili recipes call for a 6-quart, heavy-bottomed Dutch oven. It works well for boiling pasta, too.

Baking sheets, silicone pan liners, and wire cooling racks are used in my house daily, from baking cookies and cakes to roasting vegetables, to seasoning, cooking, and resting meats. I prefer the ones with a lip on the edge that prevents any items from spilling over or falling off.

Utensils

Wooden spoons work on everything from nonstick sauté pans to mixing bowls. Be sure to only hand wash and treat with care.

Kunz spoon: The standard in a professional kitchen and the most sacred spoon I own. It's the only other thing that spends as much time in my hand as my knife. Do yourself a favor: Go online and order one now. I love them so much that I give these as presents around the holidays.

Silicone spatulas, spoons, and tongs are my favorite and can go in any bowl, pan, or grill pan. They have a very high melting point and are pretty much the workhorses in my kitchen.

Fish spatula: From delicate fish to pancakes to grilling, this is my go-to for any task that requires flipping or turning.

Kitchen knife: Don't spend a fortune on a knife that you aren't going to keep sharp. A razor-sharp $20 knife beats a dull $200 one every time. Select an all-purpose blade at least 8 inches long to slice, cut, and chop animal proteins, vegetables, fruits, and herbs.

Silicone ice molds: These make variously sized cubes that will take your cocktail and beverage game to the next level. The most important things I use them for are to freeze leftover, wine, cold-brew coffee sauces, and compound butters.

Graters: The Sweet Potato Scallion Latkes recipe (page 163) requires the use of a box grater, but I use my Microplane for finely grating garlic, citrus, ginger, and Parmesan cheese.

Cutting boards: Wood is beautiful but requires intense maintenance and sanitizing. Plastic is okay but I find that my knife slips around too much on its surface. I prefer a cutting board made of natural rubber that is at least 12 x 18 inches.

Electronic Appliances

Blenders and food processors: I strongly suggest investing in a high-quality food processor and blender. The infinite amount of meals you can pull off will end up saving you thousands later.

Hand mixers and stand mixers: Many recipes call for the use of a hand or a stand mixer. There are notes where one can be substituted for the other. Otherwise I suggest that you follow the recipe suggestion.

Scales, Measuring Cups, and Spoons

Measuring devices are essential elements, especially when baking. For accuracy, I have included both weight and volume recipes for the cookie recipes on pages 228–231. If measuring by volume, make sure to level off your scoops with the backside of a knife for absolute accuracy.

Kitchen Towels and Oven Mitts

I am a big fan of the former, not so much the latter. This is a great place to save money. You can go to such places as Ikea and buy a pack of towels that cost about a dollar each. Make sure they stay completely dry, then double them over to remove hot things from the oven. If you feel more comfortable with the classic oven mitt, then make sure it is high quality and always dry.

Additional Tools to Have on Hand

Kitchen scissors	Cake tester	Disher/ice cream scoop
Spider skimmer	Thermometers for oil/meat	Plastic wrap
Mandoline	Can opener	Aluminum foil
Balloon whisk	Citrus press	Pepper mill
Basting brush	Microplane grater	Storage containers for meal prep
Salad spinner	Box grater	Popsicle molds
Colander	Y-peeler	Waffle iron
Mesh strainer	Whisk	Juicer
Rolling pin	Tongs	Nest of mixing bowls

THE ZEN OF PREP

I've always approached prep work as a meditative endeavor. I make sure that I have nothing else on the docket and all I have to worry about are the beautiful ingredients I've chosen to cook that week. The phone goes off, the music comes on, and more often than not there is a healthy pour of red wine in my glass. Here are a few tips that will have you prepping and eating like a pro.

Set yourself up for success. Sunday evening is my time to reboot and refocus on the busy week ahead. All the pots are out, the oven is cranked, and I'm in the zone of cooking and assembling a week's worth of meals.

Don't feel the need to cook all your proteins at once. I find that cooking some, marinating others, and waiting to buy delicate items, such as fish and seafood, works best with little waste.

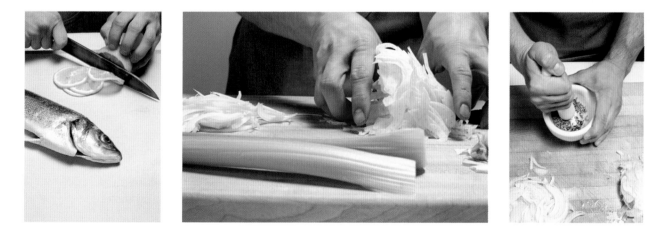

Work backwards. I always work backwards, as in start all the longer items first, such as roasted chickens, stews, sauces, quinoa, rice, nut milks, and so forth. Basically, start with anything that takes longer but doesn't require attention, which you can set and forget, leaving your focus to prep the quick-fire ingredients.

Store and prep. All my fully composed meals get stored in matching containers in the fridge and most are labeled (I use P-Touch) so I don't have to think about anything, I just read, grab, and get out the door. Other ingredients are left uncooked, but are cut and ready to be assembled into superfast suppers when I'm exhausted and don't want to bother with midweek slicing and dicing.

How to Store Food in Preparation for Cooking

Fruit: Cut everything into your desired size, lay everything flat and not touching on a tray, and freeze until solid, then place in a resealable plastic bag and store in the freezer. This eliminates the giant iceball that will form if you freeze fruit in one clump.

Vegetables: In the fridge I have vegetables in various states of prep. As soon as they come home from the market, they are all washed, dried, and stored for maximum freshness. Greens and herbs get a quick dip and rinse in a large bowl, I spin them in my salad spinner to dry, then I carefully wrap them in paper towels before placing them in labeled resealable plastic bags. This process is guaranteed to save all the delicate herbs and green items that can't withstand the cold and moist environment of your fridge.

After all my greens are safely tucked away, I start in on my other vegetables. I try to plan a few meals and chop vegetables specifically for those; I also just peel, stem, and seed some others in case I want to make something on the fly. Knowing that everything is clean and ready gives you peace of mind, and you aren't locked into a meal if you feel like mixing it up or in the event of an unexpected guest's arrival.

Herbs: Use frozen cubes for a pop of fresh flavor when you don't have fresh herbs on hand. Place in an ice cube tray, cover with extra-virgin olive oil, and freeze until solid.

Spices: It seems to be a great value to buy spices in bulk, but the reality is, if you aren't going to use them up in three to six months, they lose their punch and end up in the bin. I'm a big fan of buying the quantity of spices that matches how often you use them. Salt and pepper: Go big; you know you will use these every day. Saffron or strong curry powders, scale them back so they keep their punchy flavors.

Sauces: Fill an appropriately sized resealable plastic bag, label in permanent marker (or with a P-Touch if you are crazy like me), and place it flat on a tray to freeze. Once frozen, store upright in freezer to economize space.

Wine: It's rare for a bottle of wine in my house to go unfinished, but in the rare event that this happens: Freeze in ice cube trays and pop the cubes into a sauce or stock when you don't want to open a full bottle.

Carry-Over Ingredients

I've done my best to illustrate how to economize on all the ingredients you may buy at the market. I've made sure that these items "carry over" between multiple meals. There is nothing worse than buying a whole bunch of parsley or a huge piece of protein and not knowing how to use it for more than one recipe. No more buying a bunch of parsley, using 2 tablespoons in a recipe, and then wondering, "Now what do I do with the rest?"

BASICS TO HAVE ON HAND

If you have prepped and stored a couple of the following recipes in advance, you will be able to have a fresh, fast, and fun-to-prepare meal in minutes.

Romesco Sauce
Roasted Tomatillo Salsa
Three-Ingredient Blackberry Jam
One-Step Apricot Jam
Basic Hummus
Tahini Yogurt
Avocado Crema
Homemade Almond Butter
Almond Flour

Avocado Oil Mayo
Spicy Mayo
Paleo Crêpes
Instant Macadamia Nut Milk
Date Paste
Vanilla Almond Milk
Sweet Potato Purée
Guacamole
Cauliflower Fried Rice

No-Peanut Sauce
Basic Pizza Dough
Whole-Wheat Pasta Dough
How To: Baked Spaghetti Squash
How To: Duck
How To: Spatchcocked Chicken with
  Smoked Garlic
How To: Lobster

Romesco *Sauce*

4 large plum tomatoes
Olive oil
5 garlic cloves, unpeeled
½ cup Marcona almonds
2 jarred roasted red bell
  peppers, drained and roughly
  chopped
2 tablespoons sherry vinegar
1 teaspoon smoked Spanish
  paprika or pimentón
Salt

1 Adjust an oven rack to middle position and preheat the oven to 400°F.

2 Arrange the tomatoes in an ovenproof pan (I like to use a pie tin) and rub them with oil. Place the garlic cloves on a piece of foil, drizzle them with oil, wrap them with the foil, and set them in the pan with the tomatoes. Roast the tomatoes for about 45 minutes, or until the tomatoes are nicely charred.

3 Transfer the pan to a cooling rack, and when cool enough to handle, carefully peel and discard the skins from the tomatoes. Unwrap the garlic and pop the cloves out of their skins.

4 Place the tomatoes, garlic, almonds, peppers, vinegar, paprika, and a good pinch of salt in a blender and purée until almost smooth, scraping down the sides as necessary (I like mine a little chunky).

It's not just for chips. Make a big batch and freeze into smaller portions that can be brought out to punch up your next meat or fish recipe.

Roasted
Tomatillo Salsa

YIELD: ABOUT 3 CUPS SALSA

1½ pounds tomatillos
1 yellow onion, peeled and
  quartered
1 garlic clove, unpeeled
1 jalapeño pepper
3 tablespoons olive oil
⅔ cup fresh cilantro leaves
Juice of 1 lime
2 teaspoons salt

1 Adjust an oven rack to the topmost position (it should be about 6 inches from the broiler). Set the broiler to HIGH.

2 Rinse the tomatillos under cold water to remove the husk and sticky residue. Place the tomatillos, onion, garlic, and jalapeño in a sturdy ovenproof pan just large enough to hold them. Drizzle with the oil, making sure to coat everything well. Place under the broiler for 7 to 9 minutes, turning the vegetables as you see them start to develop a nice rich char.

3 Transfer the pan to a cooling rack. When cool enough to handle, carefully remove the skin from the garlic and the stem from the jalapeño. Transfer everything to a food processor. Add the cilantro, lime, and salt, and process until you have a beautiful chunky sauce. Use immediately or store in an airtight container in the fridge for up to 2 days.

Three-Ingredient
Blackberry Jam

YIELD: ABOUT 3 CUPS JAM

I love preserving berries in the summer when they are abundant, but I feel like every jam recipe usually involves boiling millions of jars and a lengthy process that no busy person has time or patience for.
I've limited the process and the ingredients to just a few so you will be slathering this jam on everything in under 30 minutes.

1 Stir the blackberries and agave together in a large bowl. Cover the bowl tightly with plastic wrap and allow the berries to macerate in the fridge at least 8 hours and up to overnight.

2 Place the berries and any accumulated juices in a large, high-sided sauté pan and bring to a simmer over medium heat. Add the lime juice and cook, stirring occasionally, until thick and glossy, about 20 minutes.

3 Strain the jam through a mesh strainer set over a large heat-proof bowl, making sure to smash the berries through for total extraction of the juices. Let cool to room temperature and enjoy.

4 Store the jam in an airtight container for up to 3 weeks in the fridge.

24 ounces fresh blackberries
2 cups agave nectar
Juice of 1 lime

Get your herb on! Try tossing fresh rosemary or thyme sprigs into the jam while cooking, or even some finely grated fresh ginger.
Macerating is the process of soaking the berries in sugar to draw out their natural juices and enhance the berry flavor. This works well with any fruit and really amps up the flavors and enhances the intensity of the dish.

One-Step
Apricot Jam

YIELD: ABOUT 1 CUP JAM

This simple three-ingredient, one-step jam comes together in a matter of minutes and *you will* be serving this at your next brunch. Apricots, peaches, and other stone fruits also work well here—take advantage of them while they're in season. This jam is the perfect topping for just about anything. I've thrown it on everything from toast to cakes, and used it to smother a freshly grilled pork chop.

1½ cups apricot, pitted and diced (from about 4 apricots)
2½ tablespoons coconut palm sugar
3½ tablespoons freshly squeezed lime juice, strained

1 Place all the ingredients in a large sauté pan and cook over medium-high heat, stirring occasionally, until it becomes thick and jammy, about 10 minutes. Transfer the jam to a bowl and let cool to room temperature before using.

2 Store the jam in an airtight container for up to 3 weeks in the fridge.

This will take your Sweet Cheese Blintzes (page 239) game to the next level.

Basic *Hummus*

YIELD: ABOUT 3¾ CUPS HUMMUS

I thought I'd had hummus before, until a recent trip to the Middle East
assured me I had never tasted the real thing. I was wandering around
the Arab quarter in Jerusalem and came upon a little shop that was packed
full of people at lunch. At first I had no idea what they were being
served, but I knew whatever it was, I needed it.
I stepped inside to see these humble chickpeas being transformed into a
thick, still slightly warm, velvety paste garnished with fresh herbs
and a healthy squeeze of lemon juice. I'd arrived in hummus heaven. I've
expedited the process by using canned chickpeas but haven't sacrificed any
of the big traditional flavors.

1 Place the chickpeas in a food processor and process them until a very thick paste forms; you will need to scrape down the sides and the bottom of the bowl with a rubber spatula as you go.

2 With the machine running, add the tahini, lemon juice, and garlic through the feed tube. Slowly pour in the ice water, 2 tablespoons at a time, until the desired texture is achieved. Season liberally with salt and transfer to a serving bowl or plate.

3 Drizzle with olive oil and top with za'atar and pine nuts.

2 (15-ounce) cans chickpeas, drained and rinsed
1 cup tahini paste
6 tablespoons freshly squeezed lemon juice
2 garlic cloves, minced or grated
Ice water
Salt
Olive oil
Za'atar, for garnish
Toasted pine nuts, for garnish

If you prefer, start with dried chickpeas, soaking
them overnight. Follow the package directions, then
continue with the recipe as is.

Tahini Yogurt

YIELD: ABOUT 2 CUPS YOGURT

¼ cup tahini paste
1½ cups labne or full-fat Greek yogurt
1 to 2 tablespoons olive oil
1 garlic clove, minced or grated finely on a Microplane
Cold water
Salt

Whisk together everything but the cold water and salt. Add the water, 1 tablespoon at a time, to thin out the yogurt as needed. It should be spoonable but not watery. Season with salt.

Avocado Crema

YIELD: ABOUT 1½ CUPS CREMA

1 ripe avocado, pitted
1 cup nonfat Greek yogurt
¼ cup fresh cilantro leaves, chopped (about 2 tablespoons)
Juice of 1½ limes
1 teaspoon salt
½ teaspoon ground cumin

1 Scoop the avocado into a food processor. Add the yogurt, cilantro, lime juice, salt, and cumin and pulse until smooth, scraping the bottom and sides of the bowl as needed.

2 Transfer the avocado crema to a bowl and cover with plastic wrap until ready to use. The crema will keep for up to 3 days in the fridge.

Homemade
Almond Butter

YIELD: ABOUT 2 CUPS ALMOND BUTTER

The first time I made almond butter at home, I was amazed at how much more almond flavor was retained in the final product. I was also happy to have retained the cash that it saved me by doing it myself. This isn't just almond butter—this is almond butter on steroids. I've added a good amount of healthy medium-chain triglycerides in the coconut oil, the natural sweetness of maple syrup, and just enough cinnamon to round out the flavor. You couldn't even buy this stuff if you wanted to. When you make this once, you'll wonder how you ever ate that old, overpriced separated grocery store kind.

2 cups roasted, unsalted almonds
1 teaspoon coconut oil
2 teaspoons grade B maple syrup
¼ teaspoon ground cinnamon
1 teaspoon salt

1 Place the almonds in a food processor and process until a smooth paste is formed, about 15 minutes. Pause the processor occasionally to scrape down the bottom and sides of the bowl with a rubber spatula. Pour in the coconut oil and process for 15 seconds.

2 Pour in the maple syrup, cinnamon, and salt and process for 15 seconds more.

3 Store the almond butter in an airtight container for up to a month in the fridge.

Grade B maple syrup is darker and more robust than grade A. It's great for cooking, and usually a bit cheaper, too. Store maple syrup in the fridge; it's delicate and will develop mold if left at room temperature for too long.

Almond Flour

I won't pay a fortune for something that can be easily made at home. With the reduction of gluten in many people's diet, alternative flours have become increasingly popular in recent years. And as with anything that becomes popular, the big companies want to charge you more. Almond flour is one ingredient: raw almonds, ground up. More and more, companies have been selling it for way more than the cost of what it is. With a few pulses of your food processor, you can have all the almond flour you want. The key here is to not pulse the nuts too much or else you'll end up with almond butter. It's a tasty mistake, but not what we're going for in this recipe.

1 cup blanched almonds

1 Place the almonds in a food processor and pulse until a fine powder forms.

2 If you want to get picky, you can sift the flour through a mesh sieve.

3 Store the almond flour in a resealable plastic bag for up to 2 months in the fridge.

Don't be fooled by the name: Almond flour is not like regular flour; they react very differently and you can't just substitute one for the other. I like to use almond flour in many dishes both sweet and savory, for the amazing nutty flavor and nice kick of protein. If you love almonds, try the Cherry Clafoutis Cookies (page 247).

Avocado Oil Mayo

YIELD: ABOUT 1½ CUPS MAYO

Mayonnaise is one of the original "mother sauces" and is noted for
its incredible versatility throughout many dishes and cuisines. The great
thing is that it's a blank canvas open for interpretation. Make it once as is,
then try tossing in some chopped fresh herbs or playing around with
different acids and oils. In this particular recipe I've replaced the devoid-of-
nutritional-density vegetable oil with heart-healthy avocado oil, for a big omega-3
boost. It's also flat-out delicious and a snap to make at home.
Use this creamy delicious mayo in the Tuna Snack (page 123),
and also in the Buttermilk Dressing (page 146).

1 Place the yolks, mustard, lemon juice, and salt in a food processor. Process for about 15 seconds; then, with the machine still running, start to add the oil in a slow, thin, and steady stream until it fully emulsifies to form a thick and luxurious sauce.

2 Transfer the mayo to a bowl and use immediately or store in an airtight container for up to 1 day in the fridge.

3 large egg yolks
2 teaspoons Dijon mustard
1 tablespoon freshly squeezed
   lemon juice, strained
½ teaspoon kosher salt
¾ cup avocado oil

You can go old school and whisk this mayo
by hand. Keep the bowl anchored on the counter by wrapping
a damp kitchen towel around the base. Remember, adding
the oil a small amount at a time is crucial to making a
smooth, rather than curdled, mayo.

Spicy Mayo

YIELD: ABOUT ½ CUP MAYO

Spicy mayo has become an ubiquitous condiment over the years. This is my take
on Japanese Kewpie mayo that packs a spicy punch.

Whisk all the ingredients together and store for up to a week in the fridge.

6 tablespoons Avocado Oil
   Mayo (recipe above)
4 teaspoons Sriracha
2 teaspoons mirin

Paleo *Crêpes*

This is the perfect answer for anyone who doesn't eat grains but still would love to enjoy a crêpe or tortilla. This is a base recipe that can be used as a taco, such as my Spicy Duck Tacos (page 209), to a dessert, such as the Sweet Cheese Blintzes (page 239).

2 large eggs
1 cup unsweetened almond milk
½ cup tapioca starch
3 tablespoons arrowroot powder
3 tablespoons coconut flour
½ teaspoon salt
Unsalted butter, ghee, or oil

1 Whisk the eggs in a medium-size bowl. Whisk in the almond milk. In a separate large bowl, whisk together the tapioca starch, arrowroot powder, coconut flour, and salt. Whisk the wet ingredients into the dry ingredients, mixing until no lumps remain.

2 Line a baking sheet with parchment paper.

3 Heat 1 teaspoon of butter in a medium-size, nonstick skillet over medium-high heat until bubbling or shimmering. Swirl to coat to the pan. Pour ¼ to ⅓ cup of the batter into the center of the pan and carefully and quickly swirl it around to the edges. Cook until the edges of the crêpe start to pull away from the pan, about 4 minutes.

4 Flip the crêpe and cook for another 4 minutes, or until both sides are slightly crisp.

5 Transfer to the prepared baking sheet and repeat the process until all the batter is used.

I like to place parchment between each layer of the crêpes so they don't stick together or steam.

Instant *Macadamia Nut Milk*

YIELD: ABOUT 3½ CUPS MILK

If you are in a time crunch and you can't wait to soak the almonds for almond milk, this delicious macadamia milk is done in an instant.

1 Place everything in a blender and blend until smooth, about 3 minutes.

2 Strain the milk through a fine-mesh strainer or cheesecloth into a glass jar and enjoy, or store in an airtight container for up to 5 days in the fridge.

1 cup raw macadamia nuts
3½ cups water
1 tablespoon Date Paste (recipe follows)
¼ teaspoon fine sea salt
½ cup ice cubes

The ice cubes make sure the milk doesn't heat up while blending, so you can use it straight away.

Date Paste

YIELD: ABOUT 2 CUPS DATE PASTE

This became something of an addiction when I first created it. Originally it started as an energy-rich sweetener for my Paleo Protein Balls (page 120), but then I realized it tastes pretty darn good spread on toast, as a substitute for white sugar in cookies, and in anything you want to sweeten.

2 cups dates, pitted
½ cup water
¼ teaspoon salt
¼ teaspoon ground cinnamon
(optional)

Place the dates and water in a small saucepan. Bring the mixture to a boil over medium-high heat, then remove from the heat, and cover. Allow the dates to soak for 5 minutes, or until softened. Transfer the dates, any remaining water, salt, and cinnamon to a blender or food processor and pulse until smooth. Date paste can be stored in an airtight container for up to 2 weeks in the fridge.

Vanilla Almond Milk

YIELD: ABOUT 4 CUPS MILK

When you buy this from the store, you're lucky if you get a few almonds per gallon of water, mixed with some binders, preservatives, and a bunch of other things you can't pronounce. Save yourself some cash and make a delicious rich and creamy almond beverage that has as much body as a glass of whole milk.

1 Drain and rinse the almonds. Place them in a blender with 3½ cups of fresh water and the remaining ingredients and blend for 3 minutes.

2 Strain through a nut bag or cheesecloth-lined fine-mesh colander.

1 cup blanched almonds, soaked overnight in 3 cups water

3½ cups water

1 to 2 tablespoons Date Paste (recipe above)

½ teaspoon pure vanilla extract

¼ teaspoon fleur de sel (or Kosher salt)

Save that almond meal! Spread it out on a silicone baking mat or parchment-lined sheet pan and bake at 200°F for about 2 hours, until dry. Use in the Cherry Clafoutis Cookies (page 247).

Sweet Potato Purée

YIELD: 2 CUPS PURÉE

Great for postworkout carbs and electrolytes.
If you want to reduce the sugar slightly, use half
water and half coconut juice.

3 cups thinly sliced (⅛-inch) sweet potato
2 cups coconut juice (not coconut water)
½ teaspoon kosher salt

1 Place the sweet potato slices in a medium-size lidded saucepan, cover with the coconut juice, and add the salt.

2 Bring to a boil, lower the heat to a simmer, and cook, covered, until completely softened and easily broken apart when pierced with a knife, 10 to 12 minutes.

3 Scoop out the solids into a blender and add ½ cup of the cooking liquid to start.

4 Remove the small cap from the blender lid and cover the opening with a towel.

5 Starting on low speed and gradually working to high, blend the purée until completely smooth.

6 Add more cooking liquid only if it won't blend. It's a purée, not a soup.

7 Use or freeze within 3 days.

Guacamole

Avocados are a staple in my daily diet because they are loaded with healthy fats and energy. If I hear guac is "extra" one more time, I may lose it. Skip the hassle and make it for yourself. This is supposed to be a snack, but it's so tasty I usually make it a meal.

Scoop the avocados into a large bowl, and using a whisk, start to mash the avocados to your desired texture (I like mine to be chunky). With a spoon or rubber spatula, fold in the remaining ingredients, except the chips, seasoning to taste with salt. Serve immediately.

> Spoon this over whole-wheat toast with a fried egg for a brilliant breakfast option.

3 ripe avocados, pitted
Juice of ½ orange
Juice of 1 lime
1 jalapeño pepper, ribs and seeds removed, minced
1 chipotle chile in adobo sauce, minced (optional)
¼ cup fresh cilantro leaves, chopped (about 2 tablespoons)
Salt
Oven-Baked Corn Chips (page 221)

Cauliflower
Fried Rice

YIELD: ABOUT 3 CUPS "RICE"

This is a sneaky way to get the look and feel of fried rice while maintaining a reasonable amount of carbs. It is really a fun recipe to experiment with, by adding any vegetables or flavors you desire. The key is to not make the "grains" too small and to cook them in a very hot pan so the outside gets crisp and the inside remains firm.

1 head cauliflower

2 tablespoons unsalted butter, coconut oil, or olive oil

4 to 5 scallions, ends trimmed, thinly sliced to yield ½ cup

1 tablespoon liquid aminos or tamari

1 Cut the core and leaves away from the cauliflower and discard.

2 Cut the cauliflower into 1-inch chunks and pulse them in a food processor until the cauliflower resembles short-grain rice. You may need to work in batches, depending on the size of the cauliflower.

3 Heat the oil in a large skillet over medium-high heat until it starts to shimmer. Add the "rice" and fry until crisp on the outside and tender on the inside, 3 to 5 minutes. Remove from the heat and stir in the scallions and the aminos

4 Use immediately or spread onto a sheet pan and pop in the fridge to stop the cooking.

After you cut the steaks for your Cauliflower Steak (page 149), be sure to save those scraps and use them here.

Chapter 2

Take Comfort: *Healthy Comfort Food*

The first few months after my divorce were pretty ugly. I was drinking too much, staying out too late, and definitely wasn't putting quality food in my body. I was hung out and hung over and in need of something that was comforting and didn't leave me feeling terrible.

That's when I developed my healthy approach to comfort food. Because, let's face it, food is comforting. A pile of mac and cheese, a pint of ice cream, a slice of chocolate cake—after a big disappointment, food is a natural way to make us feel better. So, if you feel like burying your face and your feelings in a whopping slice of cheesecake when there are more life changes going around than you know what to do with, do it, but do it in the right way!

Try my healthy comfort foods for all of the comfort, with less guilt tomorrow.

This chapter includes healthy recipes that will enable you to enjoy your favorites and still look and feel your best. Eat your feelings, just not forever....

Always buy tightly crack-free, fully closed shellfish. Soak them in well-salted cold water for about 10 minutes, then scrub them clean under cold running water. Remove any fibrous "beards" or dirt. Discard any shellfish that do not open during cooking.

Quick *Cioppino*

YIELD: 6 SERVINGS

This is one of my all-time favorite comfort foods. This stew is rustic and tasty with almost any type of fish. If you don't love the fishes I have chosen, feel free to sub any you may prefer. Scallops, bass, snapper, or clams would all be perfect candidates here.
If in doubt, you can always ask your local fishmonger at the market. He or she can tell you what's fresh and help you discover what you like.

Salt
¼ teaspoon red pepper flakes
¼ teaspoon fennel seeds
Extra-virgin olive oil
1 fennel bulb, fronds reserved, bulb and stems thinly sliced
½ yellow onion, thinly sliced
2 celery stalks, finely chopped
2 garlic cloves, minced
1 bunch basil, leaves picked and stems reserved
1 (15-ounce) can tomato purée
1 cup dry white wine
8 ounces red snapper or any mild white fish, skin on, pin bones removed
½ pound jumbo shrimp, peeled and deveined, tails on or off
Freshly ground black pepper
¾ pound mussels, scrubbed and beards removed
Zest of 1 lemon

1 Preheat the oven to 200°F and place six heatproof bowls inside to keep warm.

2 In a mortar and pestle, spice grinder, or blender, mash ¼ teaspoon of salt, the red pepper flakes, and the fennel seeds to a fine powder. If using a blender or spice grinder, blend on high speed in 3- to 5-second bursts. Set aside.

3 In a Dutch oven or other large, heavy-bottomed pot, heat 3 tablespoons of the oil over medium heat until shimmering. Add the fennel slices, onion, celery, garlic, basil stems, and powdered spices from step 2. Cook until softened and just beginning to turn golden brown, stirring occasionally, about 10 minutes.

4 Add the tomato purée and wine and cook, uncovered, stirring occasionally, for 10 to 12 minutes, or until thickened.

5 Lower the heat to medium-low so the sauce is at a low simmer. Lightly season the fish and shrimp with salt and pepper. Arrange them, along with the mussels, in an even layer on top of the sauce. Cover the cioppino and cook for 5 minutes, or until the fish and shrimp are opaque and the mussels have opened. Discard any unopened mussels.

6 Gently stir the cioppino and season to taste with salt and pepper. Top with torn basil leaves, lemon zest, and reserved fennel fronds.

7 Ladle into the warm bowls and serve immediately.

Wild Boar Ragu

YIELD: 6 SERVINGS

This is a perfect recipe for a lazy Sunday when time is on your side.
You start with a few ingredients and then you forget about it for a few hours,
letting it simmer and develop the most amazing rich flavors, until
you're left with a deliciously rich ragu. This recipe can be substituted with
ground beef and pork sausage if that's all you can find.

3 tablespoons olive oil

4 small carrots, peeled and finely diced

2 celery stalks, peeled and finely diced

1 large red onion, very finely diced

3 garlic cloves, grated

1½ tablespoons whole fennel seeds, ground in a spice grinder or with a mortar and pestle

1 tablespoon dried oregano

2 tablespoons tomato paste

1½ pounds wild boar sausage, casings removed

½ pound meatball mix (equal parts ground beef, pork, and veal)

Salt and freshly ground black pepper

Red pepper flakes

½ (750-milliliter) bottle dry red wine

2 (28-ounce) cans whole San Marzano tomatoes, crushed by hand

2 long hot Italian peppers, thinly sliced

3 tablespoons Worcestershire sauce

4 bay leaves

Balsamic vinegar

1 Heat the oil in a large Dutch oven or other large, heavy-bottomed pot over medium-high heat until shimmering. Add the carrots, celery, and onion, and cook until the vegetables have softened and the onion is translucent, about 5 minutes. Add the garlic, fennel seeds, and oregano, and cook until fragrant, 1 minute. Stir in the tomato paste and cook until darkened in color, 1 to 2 minutes.

2 Stir in the sausage and meatball mix, stirring and breaking up with a spoon. Season with salt and pepper and a pinch of red pepper flakes and continue to cook, stirring, until the meat has lost almost all its pink. Stir in the wine and cook until it is reduced by half, about 8 minutes. Add the tomatoes, Italian peppers, Worcestershire sauce, and bay leaves and bring everything to a boil over. Lower the heat to medium so that the sauce is just gently bubbling.

3 Cook for 2 hours, or until the sauce is your desired thickness, stirring occasionally.

4 Finish with a splash of balsamic vinegar and stir well to combine. Adjust the seasoning with salt and pepper.

Bison Stew

Bison is one of the healthiest and leanest protein sources in the animal world and also one of my favorites. Since it is so lean, I've added a little fat back into the recipe with the help of the bacon. This stew is not the traditional simmer all-day kind; you get tons of flavor on your table in about 90 minutes. If you are having trouble finding bison, cubed chuck would be a great alternative.

For the stew:

1 Cook the bacon in a large Dutch oven or heavy-bottomed pot over medium-high heat, stirring, until golden brown and crisp, about 6 minutes.

2 Stir in the onion and bell pepper and cook until the onion is translucent and the pepper is tender, about 5 minutes. Season with salt.

3 Stir in the garlic, chile powder, oregano, and chipotle chiles and sauce and cook for 2 more minutes.

4 Make a well in the center of the vegetables and add the bison.

Season with salt and pepper and cook, stirring occasionally, until the meat is no longer pink, about 8 minutes. Make sure to brown meat on all sides, if using cubed bison. Pour in the beer and simmer until it's reduced by half, about 5 minutes.

5 Add the chicken stock, tomatoes, and squash, then increase the heat to high and bring to a boil. Lower the heat to low and simmer until the squash is tender and the sauce has thickened, about 1 hour 15 minutes. Adjust the seasoning with salt and pepper.

To serve: Serve with the suggested garnishes.

If you can't find bison, chuck or any lean ground meat will do. You may find it odd that I'm using chicken stock in meat stew, but I find store-bought beef stock to have an unpleasant and tinny flavor. There are enough big flavors in here that a more neutral chicken stock works perfectly.

STEW:

3 strips bacon, thinly sliced
1 yellow onion, diced
1 yellow bell pepper, cored, seeded, and diced
Salt
4 garlic cloves, minced
6 tablespoons ancho chile powder
3 tablespoons dried oregano
2 canned chipotle chiles in adobo sauce, minced, plus 2 tablespoons adobo sauce
2½ pounds ground or cubed bison
Freshly ground black pepper
1 (12-ounce) bottle or can lager-style beer
1 quart low-sodium chicken stock
2 (28-ounce) cans diced tomatoes, drained
1 (1½ pound) butternut squash, peeled, seeded, and cut into 1-inch dice

TO SERVE:

Scallions, thinly sliced
Fresh cilantro, chopped
Greek yogurt
Avocados, thinly sliced

Butternut Squash *Lasagne*

YIELD: 6 TO 8 SERVINGS

It's always fun finding new and exciting ways to use ingredients that have become commonplace. By replacing the traditional pasta noodles with butternut squash, you increase the nutritional density, save on empty calories, and add the rich, satisfying squash flavor that everyone loves.

For the butternut squash "noodles":

1. Preheat the oven to 400°F.

2. Peel and slice the butternut squash into strips ⅛ inch thick and about 6 inches long, using a mandoline if you have one, reserving the bottoms for Bison Stew (previous recipe).

3. Toss the squash strips in just enough olive oil to coat and arrange in a single layer on sheet pans lined with parchment paper.

4. Roast for 15 minutes, or just until tender but still pliable. Remove from the oven and allow to cool.

For the balsamic caramelized onions:

1. Heat the oil over medium-high heat in a large pan, add the onions and salt, and gently toss to coat them in the oil.

2. Add the thyme and lower the heat to low. Cook, covered, for 30 to 40 minutes.

3. Once completely tender, add the balsamic and cook, covered, for another 10 minutes; the onions should be caramelized and syrupy.

4. Transfer them to a bowl and set aside.

For the garlic spinach/ricotta filling:

1. Heat the oil over medium-high heat in a large pan, add the garlic and chili flakes, and sauté until golden. Remove and discard the garlic but not the oil.

Continued . . .

BUTTERNUT SQUASH "NOODLES":
- **2 butternut squash**
- **Olive oil**

BALSAMIC CARAMELIZED ONIONS:
- **3 tablespoons olive oil**
- **3 yellow onions, thinly sliced**
- **Pinch of salt**
- **2 thyme sprigs, leaves only**
- **1 tablespoon balsamic vinegar**

GARLIC SPINACH/RICOTTA FILLING:
- **1 tablespoon olive oil**
- **1 garlic clove, thinly sliced**
- **Pinch of red pepper flakes**
- **15 ounces baby spinach leaves**
- **20 ounces part-skim ricotta cheese**
- **1 teaspoon kosher salt**

TURKEY SAUSAGE RAGU:
- **1 pound Italian turkey sausage**
- **1 tablespoon olive oil**
- **8 ounces cremini mushrooms, thinly sliced**
- **36 ounces of your favorite store-bought tomato sauce**

FOR ASSEMBLY:
- **2 ounces Parmesan cheese**

2   Add the spinach and cook just until wilted. Remove from the heat and squeeze out the excess moisture, then chop roughly.

3   In a large bowl, fold together with the ricotta, season with salt, and set aside.

For the turkey sausage ragu:

1   Remove the sausage from its casing.

2   Heat the oil in a medium-sized saucepan and brown the sausage, gently breaking it apart with the back of a spoon.

3   Using a slotted spoon, remove the meat from pan and drain onto a plate lined with paper towel, reserving the fat in the pan to cook the mushrooms.

4   Add the mushrooms and cook until nicely browned, 7 to 8 minutes. Return the turkey sausage to the pan and pour the sauce over, stirring to combine. Bring to a boil, reduce to a simmer until thickened, about 15 minutes

Assembly: Lower the oven temperature to 350°F. Using a 9 x 13-inch pan, spoon in a thin layer of sauce, add the butternut squash, slightly overlapping, then half of the caramelized onions, followed by a thin layer of the spinach/ricotta mixture, and half of the ragu, and repeat until the pan is full. Finish with a layer of sauce.

1   Bake, covered with foil, for 30 minutes.

2   Remove from the oven and grate the Parmesan over the top.

3   Allow to stand at room temperature for 5 minutes before cutting.

> If you haven't yet purchased a mandoline, I suggest you do. You will get perfectly thin slices of squash for this recipe, you'll become a julienne world champ, and you'll also have the best-looking French fries on the block.

Whole-Wheat
Pasta Dough

YIELD: 4 TO 6 PORTIONS

Three ingredients, infinite possibilities.
With the assistance of the food processor, I've taken most
of the hard work out of pasta making. I like to roll and cut the
dough into various shapes and sizes, portion, flour well,
and freeze for later use when I am in a rush.

**1½ cups stone-ground wheat
00 flour, plus more for
work surface**
3 large eggs
Salt

1 Place the flour, eggs, and salt in a food processor and process until a ball starts to form.

2 Turn out the dough onto a floured cutting board and knead with the heel of your hand for 6 to 8 minutes, or until it becomes smooth and leathery.

3 Shape the dough into a disk and wrap it tightly in plastic wrap. Allow the dough to rest at room temperature for at least 30 minutes before rolling out.

> This is enough dough for four to six portions.
> I normally double it, roll it out, and freeze cut pasta in
> portions to drop into boiling water whenever
> I want a quick dinner.

How To:
Basic Pizza Dough

YIELD: 2 (12- TO 14-INCH PIZZAS)

This is my favorite method for making pizza dough quickly without flour ending up in every nook and cranny of the house. I've taken out all the guesswork and also most of the intense kneading and rolling. All that's left now is for you to dream up the ultimate pizza party.

1½ cups 110°F water
2 teaspoons active dry yeast
2 teaspoons honey
3½ cups stone-ground wheat 00 bread flour
2 teaspoons salt
2 tablespoons olive oil, plus more for oiling the bowl

1 Mix the warm water, yeast, and honey together in a small bowl. Set on a counter to rest for 5 minutes. The mixture should get nice and foamy; if it doesn't, your yeast is dead.

2 Place the flour and salt in your food processor and pulse a few times to mix.

3 Pour the yeast mixture and olive oil over the flour and process until the dough comes together in a ball, about 45 seconds.

4 Turn out onto a floured surface and gently knead and fold the dough with the palm of your hands for about 5 minutes, forming it into a large ball.

5 Drizzle a large bowl with about 1 tablespoon of olive oil and place the dough inside, flipping the dough a few times to coat it with the oil.

6 Cover tightly with plastic wrap and place in a warm area of your kitchen to rise for about an hour.

7 After the dough has risen, punch it down in the bowl and turn it back onto your floured board.

8 Cut the dough into four pieces and wrap separately in large, resealable plastic bags. Freeze or refrigerate straight away. The dough will continue to rise if it is in the fridge, so don't be alarmed.

I make a big batch of dough and keep it in the freezer for unexpected hungry guests who seem to always show up at odd hours! I also find that the day after I make this, once it has risen again in the fridge, I have even better results.

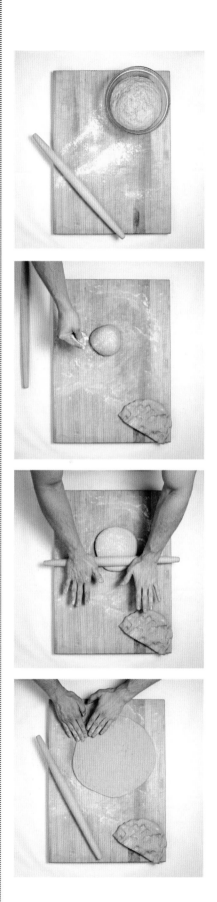

Pizza Margherita

YIELD: 2 (12-INCH) PIZZAS

I'll never forget the first time I tried to order a pizza in Italy. Being the young—read *ignorant*—American that I was at that time, I called the waiter over to take our order. "We'll have a pizza with mozzarella, prosciutto, tomato, olives and…" "*No,*" the waiter replied. "Too many toppings. I know what you want," he said, and turned and walked away. I sat there for a second, half embarrassed but mostly confused. The waiter walked past my waved hand twice and returned 10 minutes later with the most beautiful and simple pizza ever. The following is my attempt to do that brilliant man justice. Don't be tempted to add too many toppings; it only leads to soggy dough and sad pizza memories.

1 Adjust an oven rack to the middle position and preheat the oven to 500°F. If you have a pizza stone, now is the time to use it: Place it in the oven while it preheats.

2 On a well-floured board, use your fingers to press half of the dough into a flat round. Lift the dough and gently stretch it out with the back of your closed fists, until you have a 12-inch circle. Don't worry about it being too perfect; it shouldn't be. Repeat with the second half of the dough.

3 Spread about ¼ cup of tomato purée evenly over the pies, leaving about 1 inch clean at the edges. Add more if desired, but the sauce should just be a thin coating. Tear the mozzarella apart with your hands and arrange evenly over the pizzas.

4 Season evenly with Maldon salt, drizzle lightly with olive oil, and bake one at a time on the pizza stone or a well-floured, inverted sheet pan until the crust is slightly burnt and the cheese is starting to bubble, 10 to 12 minutes. Garnish with the basil and oregano leaves and serve.

All-purpose flour, for work surface
1 recipe Basic Pizza Dough (see page 52), split in half
Tomato purée
12 ounces fresh mozzarella cheese
Maldon or other flaky sea salt
Olive oil
Fresh basil leaves, for garnish
Fresh oregano leaves, for garnish

You don't need to buy "pizza sauce" from the store. A can of crushed San Marzanos or tomato purée is cheaper and more authentic.

Gluten-Free
Fig and Goat Cheese Pizza

YIELD: 1 PIZZA

I created this low-carb pizza for a friend of mine that is afflicted with celiac disease and as a result can't have any gluten in her diet. She was sad that she would never be able to enjoy pizza again, so I worked extremely hard to create one that would be as close as possible to the real thing. I went through countless iterations while experimenting, but it wasn't until I baked the dough in a springform pan that it took on the look and feel of the real deal. If gluten isn't something that bothers you, flip to page 52 and follow the simple steps to make my Basic Pizza Dough.

For the dough:

1 Adjust an oven rack to the middle position and preheat the oven to 350°F.

2 Cut the core and leaves away from the cauliflower and discard.

3 Cut the cauliflower into 1-inch chunks and pulse them in a food processor until they turn into a paste. You may need to work in batches, depending on the size of the cauliflower. Scrape the bottom and sides of the food processor with a rubber spatula as needed.

4 Scrape the paste onto a piece of cheesecloth, wrap it, and squeeze until all liquid has been wrung out. Let sit for 5 minutes inside the cheesecloth and squeeze once again to wring out any remaining liquid.

5 Transfer the cauliflower paste to a bowl and discard the cheesecloth. Stir in the eggs, cheese, thyme, and rosemary and season with salt and pepper.

6 Use the bottom of a 12-inch round, nonstick springform (cheesecake) pan to outline a circle on a large sheet of parchment paper. Cut out the circle. Spray the pan with cooking spray and line with the parchment circle. Spray the parchment with cooking spray. Scrape the cauliflower mixture into the prepared pan, patting it down with a measuring cup to form a packed and even layer.

GLUTEN-FREE "DOUGH":
- **1 medium-size cauliflower head**
- **2 large eggs, beaten**
- **2 ounces mozzarella cheese, grate**
- **1 teaspoon fresh thyme leaves**
- **½ teaspoon fresh rosemary, finely chopped**
- **Salt and freshly ground black pepper**
- **Cooking spray**

CARAMELIZED RED ONION:
- **2 tablespoons olive oil**
- **1 large red onion, thinly sliced**
- **Salt and freshly ground black pepper**

BALSAMIC SYRUP:
- **½ cup balsamic vinegar**
- **1 tablespoon pure maple syrup**

FOR ASSEMBLY:

6 medium-size figs, stemmed and sliced into ¼-inch-thick rounds

4 ounces goat cheese, broken into medium-size chunks

Carmelized Red Onion

1½ cups baby arugula leaves

Balsamic Syrup

7 Bake the dough for 35 to 45 minutes, or until beginning to brown at the edges and slightly firm to the touch.

8 Prepare the caramelized red onion and the balsamic syrup while the dough is baking.

9 When the crust is done, transfer the pan to a cooling rack, and with an oven mitt or dry dish towel, release the springform latch. Using a large metal spatula, carefully transfer the crust to a rimmed baking sheet.

For the caramelized red onion: Heat the oil over medium-high in a small skillet until shimmering. Add the onion and season with salt and pepper. Cook, stirring occasionally, for about 8 minutes, or until the onion is completely soft and caramelized. Remove from the heat.

For the balsamic syrup: Whisk together the vinegar and syrup in a small saucepan. Bring the mixture to a boil over high heat, then cook about 5 minutes, or until thick and syrupy. Remove from the heat.

Assembly: Top with the figs, goat cheese, and caramelized onion and bake for another 8 to 10 minutes. Just before serving, top with the arugula and a healthy drizzle of balsamic syrup.

> The herbed dough makes a great base for any pizza you can dream of, so feel free to dream up all sorts of combinations.

Shaved Asparagus and Gruyère *Flatbread*

YIELD: 1 FLATBREAD

4 ounces Basic Pizza Dough
  (recipe on page 52)
3 asparagus spears
2 ounces grated Gruyère
2 ounces goat cheese
Olive oil
Maldon Salt
Pepper

1 Preheat oven to 500°F.

2 Let a 4-ounce piece of dough come to room temperature.

3 Flour a prep surface and the top of the dough well and roll out to about 12 inches by 5 inches, cover with plastic wrap, and set aside.

4 Using a peeler, shave the asparagus and reserve in ice water.

5 Grate the Gruyère and break apart the goat cheese.

6 Assemble the flatbread: Remove the asparagus from the water and pat dry, sprinkle about 1 ounce of the goat cheese on the dough, followed by the asparagus, and another layer of Gruyère.

7 Drizzle with olive oil.

8 Bake on a well-floured inverted half-sheet pan for about 10–12 minutes, or until the edges and cheese are golden brown.

9 Season with salt and pepper.

Vegan Thai
Butternut Squash Soup

This soup started as a way to economize all the scraps from the
Butternut Squash Lasagne (page 49) and it has morphed into an exotic soup that
becomes a meal unto itself. The addition of such exotic ingredients
as ginger, coconut milk, and kaffir lime leaves will transport you to the beaches
of Phuket, even on the coldest winter's day.

1 Adjust an oven rack to the middle position and preheat the oven to 350°F.

2 Place the squash, onion, and carrots in a large bowl. Drizzle with olive oil until well coated, and season with salt and pepper.

3 Spread the vegetable mixture onto a sheet pan and scatter the thyme sprigs over the top. Place the pan in the oven.

4 Place the garlic cloves on a small piece of foil, drizzle with 1 teaspoon of olive oil, seal it to make a packet, and place in the oven on a separate rack.

5 Roast the vegetables for 40 to 45 minutes, stirring every 10 minutes or so, until the vegetables are softened and are easily pierced with the tip of a knife.

1 (2-pound) butternut squash, peeled, seeds and membranes removed, and coarsely chopped

1 large sweet onion, coarsely chopped

3 medium-size carrots, coarsely chopped

Olive oil

Salt and freshly ground black pepper

6 thyme sprigs

3 garlic cloves, whole

5 kaffir lime leaves

1 (2-inch) piece fresh ginger, peeled and sliced

1.5 liters vegetable stock

2 vegan bouillon vegetable stock cubes

1 (14-ounce) can light coconut milk

1 cup toasted hazelnuts (optional)

Hazelnut oil (optional)

6 Transfer the vegetables to a large Dutch oven or other heavy-bottomed pot, using a fish spatula or slotted spoon. Remove the garlic from the foil packet. Peel and discard the skin and add the cloves to the pot. Add the kaffir lime leaves, ginger, vegetable stock, stock cubes, and coconut milk and bring to a simmer over medium-high heat. Lower the heat to medium-low and simmer for 25 minutes, stirring often.

7 Remove the kaffir lime leaves and carefully purée the soup in a blender, working in batches.

8 Finish with chopped hazelnuts and a drizzle of hazelnut oil, if using.

How To:
Duck

YIELD: 1 DUCK BREAST

Duck is my dream protein and I order it anytime it appears on a menu. Fried, Peking, braised, whole, I'll take it any way I can. When I started writing this book, I polled my friends to see what foods they've always wanted to know how to cook. The overwhelming response back was, "Duck, but I'm terrified of screwing it up." I assure you if you follow the below instructions, you will come out with a perfect crisp-skinned and rosy-hued duck breast every time.

1   Start with a well-chilled duck breast. Trim any excess fat and remove the underside tendon and any silver skin.

2   Score the fat in a crosshatch pattern and season liberally with salt and freshly ground black pepper.

3   Place the duck breast, skin side down, in a large, cold skillet. Turn on the heat to medium. The fat will begin to gently render from the skin, rather than crisp. As the fat releases, spoon it into a small bowl or jar.

4   Store the fat in an airtight container for up to 2 weeks in the fridge and use it to make Duck Fat Sweet Potato Chips (page 124).

5   Cook for 10 to 15 minutes, or until the skin is dark golden and crisp. Flip the breast and sear the underside for 2 to 3 minutes. Transfer to a cutting board and allow to rest for 5 to 10 minutes before slicing and serving.

6   For medium rare: The bottom side of the duck should feel like the fleshy part of your hand when you touch your thumb to your index finger.

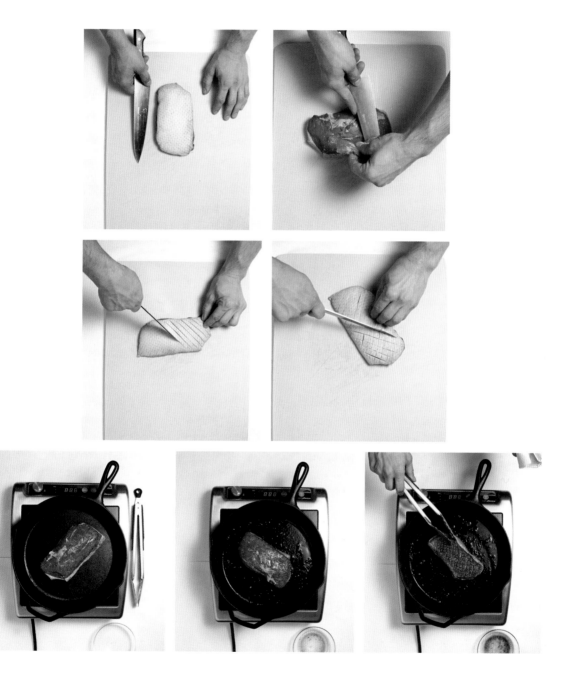

Duck Fried Rice

YIELD: 2 CUPS RICE

This is one of those recipes I like to make in large batches and pop out whenever I'm in need of a quick meal. The options for topping this whole-grain protein and vitamin-rich rice are endless.

1 Place the rice in a fine-mesh sieve and rinse under cold water until it runs clear. Shake the sieve to drain and set aside.

2 Heat the olive oil in a large saucepan over medium-high heat until shimmering. Add the onion and salt and cook until tender, about 5 minutes. Add the shiitakes and thyme and continue to cook, stirring occasionally, until the mushrooms have released most of their liquid, 3 to 5 minutes.

3 Stir in the rice and continue to cook for about 2 minutes, stirring to lightly toast the rice. Add the stock and salt and bring to a boil, then lower the heat to low. Cover the pot and cook for about 45 minutes, or until the rice is tender and fluffy.

4 Turn off the heat, but do not uncover the pot. Allow the rice to rest for 15 minutes. Fluff with a fork and serve, or continue with this recipe.

5 Top with the sliced duck and sliced scallions and serve with tamari sauce.

1 cup long-grain brown rice
3 tablespoons olive oil
1 Spanish onion, finely diced
½ teaspoon salt
3 ounces shiitake mushrooms, stems removed, tops thinly sliced
1 teaspoon fresh thyme leaves
2½ cups homemade or low-sodium chicken or vegetable stock
½ teaspoon salt
1 breast of duck, thinly sliced (see How To: Duck, page 62)
2 scallions, thinly sliced
Tamari sauce

Cooked rice may be stored
in an airtight container for
up to 3 days in the fridge.
If you want a duck-free option, try
this recipe with a big spoonful of
my Kale Walnut Pesto (page 115)
and top with a fried egg.

Lamb Kofta

YIELD: 2 TO 4 SERVINGS

When I started to mix the ingredients together for kofta, the heady smells took me right back to the *shouk* in the Arab quarter of Jerusalem where I first saw this being made. I remember saying to my wife, "Everything that is great about this guy's shop would be completely illegal in America." Bare-handed, the owner was mixing a giant pile of lamb, herbs, and spices piled high on a huge marble slab that abutted the walkway. He smiled at me and before he could even get the word *welcome* from his lips, I was seated and pointing politely and nodding my head yes to whatever he was about to say.

The pita came, warm of course, then the plates of lamb. Nothing fancy here: charred lamb, onion, and tomato on a Styrofoam plate. It was so good, I didn't know whether to kiss him or punch him out of jealousy that I could never re-create this in my own home. I ended up thanking him graciously, and my wife's beautiful blue eyes and broken Arabic landed me a small bag of spices that to this day I can't distinguish: a mix of cinnamon and nutmeg and allspice, I know, but in what quantities are a mystery to me. All I know is it didn't last long in my house and I did my best to replicate those flavors here.

Hummus is a matter of national pride and just like pasta in Italy, whoever is making it says theirs is the best. I use a very simple shortcut version (page 30) that will save you the overnight soaking of the chickpeas. If you feel inclined to soak, by all means soak it up! I was particularly hungry when I started writing the recipe, so needless to say, my stomach heavily influenced my decision.

KOFTA:
- 1 pound ground lamb
- 1 teaspoon salt
- ¼ teaspoon ground allspice
- ¼ teaspoon ground cinnamon
- ⅛ teaspoon freshly grated nutmeg
- 1 garlic clove, minced
- 1 yellow onion, chopped
- 2 tablespoons pine nuts, lightly toasted and roughly chopped
- ½ cup fresh mint leaves, roughly chopped
- ¼ cup fresh flat-leaf parsley, roughly chopped
- 1 large egg, beaten
- 3 tablespoons grapeseed oil or any high-heat oil

HERB YOGURT SAUCE:
- 1 cup Greek yogurt
- 2 large mint leaves, chopped (about 1 teaspoon)
- 4 fresh flat-leaf parsley leaves, chopped (about 1 teaspoon)
- 1 garlic clove, minced
- 1 tablespoon freshly squeezed lemon juice
- Salt
- Water, if needed

TO SERVE:
- Whole-wheat or plain pita pockets
- Basic Hummus (page 30)

For the kofta:

1. In a large bowl, combine the lamb, salt, allspice, cinnamon, nutmeg, and garlic, being careful not to overwork the meat. Add the onion, pine nuts, mint, parsley, and egg and stir to combine. Using your hands, mold the lamb into roughly 4-inch torpedo shapes and set aside. (They can be made a day in advance and kept in the fridge, tightly wrapped in plastic wrap.

2. Heat the oil over medium-high heat until just beginning to smoke. Cook the kofta until golden brown on all sides, then lower the heat to medium and continue to cook for about 5 minutes.

For the herb yogurt sauce: Whisk the yogurt, mint, parsley, garlic, and lemon juice in a small bowl. Set aside for 10 minutes to let the flavors combine. Season with salt and adjust the consistency with water if desired.

To serve: Cut the pitas in half and stuff the pockets with the hummus, herb yogurt sauce, and kofta.

Strip Steaks
with Blackberry Pan Sauce

YIELD: 2 TO 4 SERVINGS

Strip steak is the workhorse of the meat world. It doesn't get all the glory that the filet and rib eye do, but it also costs considerably less, making it a flavorful and economical option for a middle-of-the-week meal. I love repurposing ingredients as much as I can, which is why I've taken the simple blackberry jam and made it into a quick and flavorful pan sauce. Feeling that you don't have time to make a hearty meal? This goes from fridge to table in about 15 minutes, problem solved.

2 (½-pound) strip or rib steaks, preferably grass-fed

Salt and freshly ground black pepper

Olive oil

¼ teaspoon arrowroot powder

½ cup dry red wine

2 tablespoons Three-Ingredient Blackberry Jam (page 28)

1 small rosemary sprig

2 small thyme sprigs

1 garlic clove, smashed

1 tablespoon unsalted butter

1. Place the steaks on a large plate and season them generously with salt and pepper. Let them sit on the counter for at least 30 minutes before cooking.

2. Heat a large, cast-iron or other heavy-bottomed skillet over medium-high heat for at least 10 minutes.

3. Drizzle just enough oil to coat both sides of meat and carefully place in the pan, making sure to press the meat into the pan to ensure an even crust.

4. After 2 minutes, flip the steaks, and cook 2 minutes more on the opposite side. Turn the steaks so the fat side is down and lean them against the side of the pan to render out the fat cap for 1 minute.

5. Place the steaks back flat in the pan and continue to cook for 2 minutes more per side. Transfer steaks to a large, clean plate and let them rest.

6. In a small bowl, whisk the arrowroot powder into the wine.

7 Pour out the excess oil from the pan and tip in the red wine mixture, jam, rosemary, thyme, and garlic and cook, whisking constantly, until reduced by half, 3 to 4 minutes.

8 Discard the herbs and garlic and remove from the heat. Whisk in the cold butter until nicely emulsified and thick.

9 Stir in any resting juices from the steaks.

10 Slice into generous ½-inch slices and top with a nice drizzle of sauce.

Cocoa and Coffee–Encrusted
Rib Eye Steak

YIELD: 2 SERVINGS

The moment you realize that you don't have to go out and shell out a small fortune for an amazing steak dinner is one of the most liberating feelings on earth. Not only do you have a bunch of extra cash in your pocket, you get to show off your fancy new steak-making skills to all your friends.

This goes well with the
Lemon and Herb–
Roasted Sunchokes
(page 216)
for a meat-and-potatoes
kind of feel.

For the cocoa and coffee rub: In a mortar and pestle, spice grinder, or blender, mash the peppercorns, salt, espresso, and cacao to a fine powder. If using a blender or spice grinder, blend on high speed in 3- to 5-second bursts. Set aside.

For the steak:

1. Allow the steaks to sit out at room temperature for 30 minutes prior to cooking. Meanwhile, adjust an oven rack to the middle position and preheat the oven to 500°F. Set a wire rack inside a rimmed baking sheet.

2. Generously coat the meat on all sides with the rub, pressing with fingers to adhere.

3. Heat 3 tablespoons of oil in a large, heavy skillet over high heat until it begins to smoke. Add the steaks and cook for 2 to 3 minutes on each side, until a nice crust develops.

4. Add the butter, rosemary, and garlic to the pan and tip the pan toward you to allow the butter to pool. With a soup spoon, gently baste the meat for about 30 seconds.

5. Transfer the steaks to the prepared rack and cook in the oven for 4 to 5 minutes for medium rare, flipping the meat halfway through. Check for doneness with a meat thermometer, if needed, and allow the meat to rest on a cutting board for 5 to 10 minutes prior to serving.

6. Serve with the pan sauce.

COCOA AND COFFEE RUB:

- **1 tablespoon black peppercorns**
- **1 teaspoon salt**
- **1 teaspoon espresso powder**
- **1 tablespoon cacao nibs**

STEAK:

- **2 (8 ounce) ribeye steaks**
- **High-heat cooking oil, such as grapeseed or ghee**
- **2 tablespoons unsalted butter, cut into 4 pieces**
- **Leaves from 1 rosemary sprig**
- **1 garlic clove, smashed**

No-Peanut Sauce

This is a great option for anyone who is allergic to or staying away from peanut-based sauces.

Place the almond butter, coconut milk, aminos, garlic, ginger, chile, tamarind paste, fish sauce, vinegar, and lime juice in a blender and blend until smooth, scraping down the bottom and sides as needed. The sauce may be stored in an airtight container in the fridge for up to 2 weeks.

¼ cup smooth almond butter

¼ cup coconut milk

1 tablespoon coconut aminos

1 garlic clove, minced

1 (½-inch piece) fresh ginger, finely grated (1 teaspoon)

½ Thai chile, minced

1 teaspoon tamarind paste

½ teaspoon Asian fish sauce (I use Red Boat)

½ teaspoon rice vinegar

Juice of 1 lime

Paleo
Pad Thai

YIELD: 2 SERVINGS

When going strict Paleo as I mostly do, I really noticed the lack of anything that felt like an authentic Asian noodle dish. When I discovered Miracle Noodle Shirataki Angel Hair Pasta, I was amazed at how closely they mimic actual angel hair. These noodles have zero carbs, are loaded with fiber, and are gluten and soy free. They really are a miracle!

1 tablespoon coconut oil

1 garlic clove, minced

1 (½-inch piece) fresh ginger, finely grated (1 teaspoon)

½ pound medium shrimp, peeled and deveined

½ bell pepper, seeds and ribs removed, very thinly sliced

1 carrot, peeled and very thinly sliced

2 scallions, very thinly sliced

1 (7-ounce) package Miracle Noodle Shirataki Angel Hair Pasta, drained, rinsed and dried

¼ cup No-Peanut Sauce (previous recipe)

Fresh cilantro leaves, chopped, for garnish

Crushed cashews or macadamia nuts, for garnish

Lime wedges, for garnish

1. Heat the oil in a large skillet over medium-high heat until shimmering. Add the garlic and ginger and cook until fragrant, about 30 seconds. Toss in the shrimp and cook for about 3 minutes, or until beginning to turn opaque. Stir in the pepper, carrot, scallions, and noodles, and sauté for 1 more minute.

2. Add the sauce and toss to combine. Serve immediately, topped with cilantro, crushed nuts, and a squeeze of lime.

Make this Chicken Pad Thai by using the pulled meat from a Spatchcocked Chicken (see page 142).

Chapter 3
Mood Boosters:
Feel-Better Drinks and Elixirs

Everybody knows that bourbon is perfect for drowning your sorrows. Not everybody knows, however, that some herbs, elixirs, and drinks have been used for centuries to have a positive impact on moods and emotions … and liquor is just one of them. Lavender is calming and chia seeds are used by Tarahumara distance runners for the energy rush. Shakes make everybody feel good—especially if you make them with healthy ingredients.

When I need a mood boost, I turn to a good ol' jolt of caffeine. Preworkout caffeine has been proven to help your mind stay alert and helps with your fine motor skills as well. This keeps you working out longer, harder, and with more control of your movements. Just make sure you don't overdo it or it can also leave you shaky and with a stomach ache.

NOLA
Iced Coffee

YIELD: ABOUT 3 CUPS COLD BREW, FOR 6 SERVINGS OF ICED COFFEE

If you've ever tried to get your caffeine buzz on in the Deep South in the height of a sweltering summer, than you know all too well the importance of a nice strong iced coffee. Go easy your first time, as the concentrate can pack quite a punch for those sensitive to caffeine.

COLD BREW CONCENTRATE:

- **1 cup Café du Monde, New Orleans–style ground coffee**
- **3½ cups filtered water**

PER SERVING OF ICED COFFEE:

- **1 tablespoon grade B maple syrup**
- **¾ cup ice**
- **½ cup Cold Brew Concentrate**
- **½ to ¾ cup full-fat coconut milk**

For the cold brew concentrate:

1. Place the coffee grounds in the bottom of a large French press or jar. Stir in the water and let stand overnight on the counter.

2. Press the plunger down if using a French press. If using a jar, strain the coffee through a mesh colander lined with cheesecloth into a second jar. Store in the fridge until needed.

For the iced coffee:

1. Pour the syrup in the bottom of a large glass and top with the ice.

2. Stir in the cold brew concentrate and the coconut milk. Serve immediately.

This is my take on traditional NOLA iced coffee, but feel free to replace the maple syrup with any of the syrups in this book for a totally different experience.

For best results, use
a silicone mold for
your cubes. This type of mold
is indestructible and
ensures the cubes pop out
easily and cleanly.

Frozen
Lavender Latte

YIELD: 1 SERVING

I hate watered-down coffee, so I created a drink that gets better
and stronger as it sits. The slightly warm almond milk gently coaxes the
superconcentrated coffee from its frozen hibernation. The
result is a perfectly balanced summer pick-me-up.

COLD BREW CUBES:

**1 cup medium- to dark-roasted
coffee beans, ground**

3½ cups filtered water

PER SERVING OF LATTE:

2 or 3 Cold Brew Cubes

**1¼ cups unsweetened almond
milk, slightly warmed**

**2 tablespoons Lavender Simple
Syrup (recipe below)**

For the cold-brew cubes:

1. Place the coffee grounds in the bottom of a large French press or jar. Pour in the water, stir, and let stand overnight at room temperature.

2. Press the plunger down if using a French press. If using a jar, strain the coffee through a mesh colander lined with cheesecloth into a second jar.

3. Pour the cold brew into ice cube trays and freeze until solid.

For the latte: Place the cold brew cubes in a tall glass. Add the almond milk and simple syrup. Stir and enjoy.

Lavender Simple Syrup

YIELD: ABOUT 1½ CUPS SYRUP

1 cup agave nectar or honey

1 cup water

**2 tablespoons culinary-grade
lavender buds**

1. Whisk the agave and water together in a small saucepan. Stir in the lavender and bring to a boil over medium-high heat, then lower the heat to medium and simmer for 10 minutes.

2. Remove the saucepan from the heat and cover tightly with a lid or foil. Allow to come to room temperature, at least 4 hours.

3. Once cool, strain the syrup through a fine-mesh sieve into a glass bottle or jar. Use immediately or store in an airtight container for up to 2 weeks in the fridge.

Dirty Chai *Smoothie*

YIELD: 1 TO 2 SERVINGS

Is it coffee, tea, or a smoothie? Yes. The exotic flavors of India
paired with the punch of Italian espresso and omega-3-loaded hemp
seeds are a great start to any day.

1 In a small saucepan, bring the almond milk to a simmer over medium heat. Remove from the heat, add the tea bags, and allow to steep for 10 minutes. Remove and discard the tea bags and chill the chai mixture completely in the fridge.

2 Place the chai mixture, espresso, hemp seeds, honey, cinnamon, and ice in a blender and blend until smooth. Serve immediately.

1½ cups Vanilla Almond Milk (page 38)
2 chai tea bags
1 shot brewed espresso
2 tablespoons hemp seeds
½ teaspoon honey
¼ teaspoon ground cinnamon
½ cup ice

If it's late in the afternoon, I usually omit the espresso shot, so it doesn't interfere with my sleep.

80 EAT YOUR HEART OUT

Postworkout
Coffee Break

YIELD: 1 SERVING

I don't always have time to sit down to have breakfast,
so I came up with an all-in-one solution. This gets my brain fired
and focused after a hard morning workout.

1¼ cups unsweetened almond milk

1 scoop chocolate protein powder

1 scoop branched-chain amino acids

2 tablespoons chia seeds

1 shot brewed espresso

1½ tablespoons smooth almond butter

1 tablespoon raw cocoa powder

½ cup ice

Place all the ingredients in a blender and blend until smooth. Enjoy immediately.

A little bit of caffeine after a hard workout helps me feel energized again. The chia seeds and branched-chain amino acids are crucial in the repair and recovery of heavily worked muscle fibers.

Hawaii 5-0
Smoothie

YIELD: 1 SERVING

Place all the ingredients in a blender and blend until smooth. Serve immediately.

1¼ cups almond milk
½ cup frozen mango chunks
¼ cup raw coconut flakes
1 banana, peeled and sliced

From left to right: Cucumber Mint Water, Beet Down, Strawberry Balsamic Sunrise, Hawaii 5-0 Smoothie, Green Dragon Smoothie, Cucumber Mint Water, Strawberry Balsamic Sunrise

Cucumber Mint Water

YIELD: 4 SERVINGS

This is the water for people who don't like drinking water.
It's so refreshing and cooling that it tricks you into getting
those eight required glasses down while feeling as if you are
waiting for a massage at some fancy spa.

4 cups water
½ cucumber, thinly sliced
6 to 8 fresh mint leaves
½ cup ice
1 tablespoon freshly squeezed
**   lemon or lime juice (optional)**

1 Place all the ingredients in a blender
and blend until smooth.

2 Strain through a mesh strainer
(optional).

Strawberry Balsamic Sunrise

YIELD: 1 SERVING

I got this inspiration from a classic Italian dessert that includes fresh strawberries macerated in sugar, then topped with tangy balsamic. The natural sweetness of the berries with the pleasant tartness of the vinegar makes an amazing morning eye-opener.

1 Place the strawberries and almond milk in a blender and blend on high speed until smooth.

2 Add the protein powder and balsamic vinegar and blend on low speed until fully combined.

1 cup frozen strawberries
12 ounces almond milk
2 scoops vanilla protein powder
1 tablespoon balsamic vinegar

Smoothies are transportable liquid energy. They are the perfect option when sitting down for breakfast is not one. The variations are endless and I encourage you to use these recipes as a template for hundreds of your own variations. I also encourage you to invest in a high-powered blender that is powerful enough to make everything from delicious frozen drinks to silky smooth soups and purées.

Blueberry Collard *Smoothie*

YIELD: 2 SERVINGS

Collard greens haven't gotten all the fancy hype that kale has
over the last few years, but that shouldn't deter you. This cousin of broccoli
and cabbage packs a huge amount of vitamins A, C, and K and
costs a fraction of its flashy kale counterpart.

1 cup frozen mango cubes
2 handfuls raw collard greens
1 cup fresh or frozen
  blueberries
½ cup grapefruit juice
2 cups coconut water
1 scoop vanilla protein powder

Place the mango, collard greens, blueberries, grapefruit juice, and coconut water in a blender and blend until smooth. Add the protein powder and blend on low speed just to incorporate. Serve immediately.

Don't judge a book by its cover. Once blended, this isn't the
sexiest-looking smoothie, but all the antioxidants are
sure to make you feel sexier!
I always add my protein powder last and blend on low speed,
so it doesn't become an overaerated frothy mess.

Chocolate Avocado Smoothie

YIELD: 1 SERVING

Place all the ingredients in a blender and blend until smooth. Serve immediately.

> This smoothie is loaded with tons of potassium and monounsaturated fats, making it a perfect breakfast replacement or postexercise recovery drink.

1½ cups coconut water
2 kale leaves, stemmed and chopped (about 1 cup)
1 tablespoon raw cacao powder
½ avocado, peeled and pitted
½ cup frozen pineapple
2 tablespoons hemp seeds

Tropical *Greens*

YIELD: 1 SERVING

Place all the ingredients, except the coconut flakes, in a blender and blend until smooth. Top with the raw coconut flakes.

> Cut peeled, ripe bananas into bite-sized chunks and freeze them to add to your smoothies instead of ice.

¼ cup mango
¼ cup frozen banana
1 cup kale, stemmed and roughly chopped
1 tablespoon coconut oil
10 to 12 ounces coconut water
1 tablespoon hemp seeds
Raw coconut flakes, for garnish

Cherry-Almond
Protein Smoothie

YIELD: 1 SERVING

This is my go-to smoothie when I want all the flavors of a bowl of oatmeal in a portable, protein-packed smoothie.

Place all the ingredients in a blender and blend until smooth. Serve immediately.

1 tablespoon Homemade Almond Butter (page 32)
½ cup frozen cherries
2 tablespoons chia seeds
2 tablespoons hemp seeds
3 tablespoons gluten-free, old-fashioned rolled oats
1¼ cups almond milk

Watermelon Chia
Agua Fresca

This is the best flavored water that is also rich in omega-3 healthy fats and fiber.

3 cups seedless watermelon, diced
2 to 3 tablespoons Basil Lime Simple Syrup (page 188)
2 cups water
1 tablespoon chia seeds (optional)
Ice
Lime slices, for garnish

1. In a blender, blend the watermelon and water together with the syrup.

2. Pour into a large pitcher and stir in the chia seeds, if using, then refrigerate for 4 hours or overnight, stirring occasionally to break up the seeds.

3. Serve over ice with 1 lime slice per glass.

Immunity

YIELD: 1 SERVING

When I get the slightest feeling that I'm getting sick or I'm just feeling plain rundown, I make a big batch of Immunity. This isn't for the faint of heart, but the spiciness will get your body and mind back on the right track. Beets have been shown to reduce blood pressure and lessen fatigue, so embrace these garnet-hued root gems.

Run all the ingredients through a juicer. Strain through a mesh colander into a glass jar and enjoy immediately, or store in an airtight container for up to 2 days in the fridge. If storing, shake to reincorporate before drinking.

6 carrots, scrubbed
3 celery stalks, scrubbed
2 (1-inch) pieces fresh ginger
3 (1-inch) pieces fresh turmeric
1 Granny Smith apple, scrubbed
and quartered

This works great frozen in Popsicle molds to soothe a sore throat.

Turmeric Tea

This is a great tea to reduce inflammation in the body and is the perfect caffeine-free way to enjoy a warm digestive beverage after a meal.

2 cups water
1 (1-inch) piece fresh turmeric, peeled and finely grated
1 (1-inch) piece fresh ginger, peeled and finely grated
1 teaspoon honey
Pinch of sea salt
Vanilla Almond Milk (page 38)

1 Bring the water, turmeric, and ginger to a boil in a small pot.

2 Lower the heat to a simmer and cook for 10 minutes.

3 Strain into a teacup or mug and add the honey, salt, and a splash of almond milk.

This tea is also great cold over ice on a hot day.

Beet Down

YIELD: 4 TO 6 (8-OUNCE) SERVINGS

We've all been to the dark place where we just feel sluggish and beat down. This is the greatest pick-me-up I know of to date. This garnet-colored goodness is loaded with vitamins and antioxidants known to kick-start your body back to its original awesome self.

1 Run all the ingredients through a juicer. Strain the juice through a fine-mesh sieve into a large jar or carafe.

2 Drink immediately or store in an airtight container for up to 3 days in the fridge. Whisk or shake in a storage container to reincorporate prior to drinking.

3 Granny Smith apples, scrubbed and quartered
6 beets, scrubbed and quartered
1 (2-inch) piece fresh turmeric
1 (1-inch) piece fresh ginger
3 celery stalks

Beets are a nitrate-rich, high-performance fuel and have been known to increase muscular endurance over the course of maximum exertion.

Green Dragon Smoothie

YIELD: 1 SERVING

1 cup roughly chopped kale
  leaves
¼ cup frozen mango chunks
¼ cup frozen pineapple chunks
¼ avocado, peeled and pitted
2 tablespoons hemp seeds
1¼ cups coconut water

Place all the ingredients in a blender and blend until smooth. Serve immediately.

Banana-Nut-Ginger *Smoothie*

YIELD: 1 SERVING

½ cup frozen banana
3 tablespoons walnuts
1 teaspoon honey
½ teaspoon grated fresh ginger
¼ teaspoon ground cinnamon
1¼ cups Vanilla Almond Milk
  (page 38)
½ cup ice (optional)

Place all the ingredients in a blender and blend until smooth. Serve immediately.

Part Two:
Eat Well
Every Day

Creamy Scrambled Eggs with
Smoked Salmon and Herbs

Chapter 4

Fresh Start:
Single-Serving Breakfasts

Don't hate me, but I'm a morning person. When I was just starting out in culinary school, there was something so magical about waking up at the crack of dawn. It gave me a very quiet and productive time to reflect on what I had ahead of me and helped me focus on what goals I wanted to accomplish that day. No meal is more important to me than breakfast. What I fueled up on for breakfast is directly linked to how my day will go. I can't control what will bombard me as I walk out my front door, but I can do everything in my power to make sure that I'm ready to react to whatever life may throw at me. Although my mornings are extremely productive, and head clearing, I can't run solely on a cup of coffee for too long. I need fast, fit breakfasts to start off on a fresh, energized, balanced foot. No "hangryness" allowed!

Eating nutrient-dense meals help me do just that.

No-cook breakfasts, such as my Basic Muesli (page 103), will let whoever likes a few more minutes in the morning get that restorative shut-eye while still having time for a healthy and energizing morning meal.

I make these by the batch and then
freeze half to be reheated on a day
when I'm in a hurry but still want
an amazing breakfast.

Gluten-Free
Buckwheat Pancakes

YIELD: ABOUT 12 PANCAKES (DEPENDING ON SIZE)

Aside from eggs, pancakes are my favorite breakfast food. The only problem is they aren't usually nutritionally dense. I've combined some pretty awesome gluten-free powerhouse alternatives that load up these pancakes with healthy slow-digesting carbs that will keep you fueled all morning long.

PANCAKES:
- **1¼ cups almond milk**
- **1 teaspoon freshly squeezed lemon juice**
- **1 large egg, beaten**
- **½ teaspoon pure vanilla extract**
- **½ cup buckwheat flour**
- **¼ cup coconut flour**
- **¼ cup quinoa flour**
- **1 tablespoon unrefined cane sugar**
- **1 teaspoon baking powder**
- **1 teaspoon baking soda**
- **½ teaspoon salt**
- **1 tablespoon unsalted butter**

TO SERVE:
- **Fruit of your choice**
- **Ginger Maple Butter (page 177)**

For the pancakes:

1. If making pancakes for a crowd, adjust the oven rack to the middle position and preheat the oven to 200°F. Place a rimmed baking sheet in the oven.

2. In a medium-size bowl, stir together the almond milk and lemon juice. Set aside for 5 minutes, then whisk in the beaten egg and vanilla. Set aside.

3. In a large bowl, whisk together the buckwheat, coconut, and quinoa flours, the sugar, baking powder, baking soda, and salt. Pour in the almond milk mixture and stir just to combine: The batter is meant to be slightly thicker than standard pancake mix, so don't freak out!

4. Melt the butter in a medium-size nonstick skillet over medium heat, swirling around to just coat the bottom of the pan. Tip any excess butter into the batter and stir to combine.

5. Pour the batter in ⅛-cup increments into the pan, being careful not to crowd the pancakes. Cook for 2 to 3 minutes on the first side. Once the bubbles have formed and the edge has gone from wet to set and matte, give them a flip and continue to cook for about another 2 minutes. Transfer the cooked pancakes to the baking sheet in the oven and continue making pancakes with the remaining batter.

To serve: Serve with the suggested accompaniments.

Grain-Free
Protein Granola

YIELD: ABOUT 6 CUPS GRANOLA

Granola used to be a healthy, energizing breakfast. But over the years
with the prevalence of ultrarefined sugars, it's become something
closer to dessert. This recipe brings me back to the granola my grandma used to
make. Filled with heart-healthy nuts and seeds and just a touch of
natural sugar, this will keep you going all day without the afternoon carb crash.

1 cup raw almonds

1 cup raw cashews

1 cup raw pecans

**1 cup raw pepitas (pumpkin
seeds)**

1 cup raw (shelled) pistachios

1 cup raw coconut flakes

⅓ cup extra-virgin olive oil

⅓ cup pure maple syrup

**1 tablespoon coconut palm or
muscovado sugar**

1 teaspoon salt

**½ cup dried sour cherries,
roughly chopped**

1 Adjust an oven rack to the middle position and preheat the oven to 300°F. Line a rimmed baking sheet with a silicone baking mat or parchment paper.

2 Place the almonds, cashews, pecans, pepitas, and pistachios in a food processor and pulse seven times, or until it takes on a gravel-like texture. Transfer the mixture to a large bowl. Stir in the coconut flakes.

3 In a small saucepan, heat the oil, syrup, sugar, and salt over medium heat, whisking until the sugar has completely dissolved.

Pour the mixture over the nuts and stir with a spatula until they are evenly coated.

4 Spread the nut mixture on the prepared baking sheet and bake for 50 minutes, stirring every 10 minutes, until the granola is golden brown and toasty. Transfer the baking sheet to a cooling rack and stir in the cherries.

5 Allow the granola to cool completely and enjoy. The granola can be stored for up to 1 week in an airtight container at room temperature.

Coconut Chia Pudding

YIELD: ABOUT 2 CUPS PUDDING

Thanks to my vegan friends, I've been riding the chia train for quite a while, but this is the first recipe that I have really fallen in love with. It's so simple you have to at least try it once! I've been inhaling this chia pudding for breakfasts, snacks, and desserts. This ratio of chia to liquid produces a beautiful, rice pudding–like texture.

1 Place the syrup a large bowl and whisk in a small amount of the almond milk, until fully incorporated. Whisk in the remaining almond milk, the coconut milk, chia seeds, cinnamon, and the smallest pinch of salt.

2 Cover the bowl tightly with plastic wrap and place it in the fridge for at least 4 hours, whisking every 1 hour. The best results are overnight, especially if making multiple batches for breakfast or for a healthy dessert.

2 tablespoons pure maple syrup
1 cup unsweetened almond milk
1 cup unsweetened coconut milk
¼ cup chia seeds
¼ teaspoon ground cinnamon
Salt

In addition to being loaded with tons of heart-healthy omega-3 oils, these mighty seeds pack 11 grams of dietary fiber per ounce.

Basic *Muesli*

YIELD: ABOUT 5 CUPS MUESLI

I love oats, but early-morning cooking is not always an option for me.
That's why I make a big batch of this base every week and never have to worry
about missing breakfast when I'm on the go. I always wait until
just before eating to add whatever toppings I'm feeling like that day.

MUESLI BASE:
- **2 cups old-fashioned rolled oats**
- **2 cups unsweetened almond milk**
- **½ cup kefir**
- **½ cup dried cherries, roughly chopped**
- **1 banana, grated on a box grater**
- **½ apple, grated on a box grater**

TO SERVE:
- **Fresh raspberries**
- **Fresh blueberries**
- **Fresh strawberries**
- **Chopped hazelnuts**
- **Chopped pistachios**

For the muesli base: In a large bowl, stir together the oats, milk, kefir, dried cherries, banana, and apple. Cover with plastic wrap and place in the fridge overnight.

To serve: Serve the muesli with assorted fresh berries and chopped nuts.

> Rolled oats are low on the glycemic scale and will help you power through even the busiest of days.

Smoked Salmon Schmear

YIELD: 4 SERVINGS

I'm a huge fan of the schmear. I am not a huge fan when I ask for one and I get something that is 99 percent heavy cream cheese and 1 percent flavor. I've lightened the usual recipe by combining nonfat Greek yogurt and labne. This spread is all killer and no filler. I've used just enough dairy to gently blanket the generous amount of smoked salmon.

If you don't know your labne, here's the 411. Labne is a staple of most Middle Eastern diets, usually consumed at breakfast or combined with herbs and spices to be eaten as a meze for lunch and dinner. It's strained the same way that most Greek yogurts are, but labne uses a culture called kefir as the agent to separate the curds from the whey. *Whey is that important?*, you ask (sorry, couldn't resist). The finished product is thick like cream cheese, with an unbelievable tanginess. You'll never want cream cheese again!

½ cup fat-free Greek yogurt

1½ tablespoons labne

1 tablespoon capers, brine reserved

Finely grated zest and juice of ½ lemon

2 scallions, green parts only, chopped (1 tablespoon)

3 ounces smoked salmon, roughly chopped

Sprouted-grain English muffins, toasted

Juniper Salt (page 219)

1 Place the yogurt, labne, capers and brine, lemon zest and juice, and scallions in a medium-size bowl and combine, using a rubber spatula. Fold in the salmon and let stand for at least 30 minutes.

2 Spread on toasted English muffins, sprinkled with a pinch of juniper salt.

Throw in a little spinach and this makes an amazing meal-on-the-go tucked inside my Paleo Crêpe (page 35).

Bacon and Egg Baskets

YIELD: 6 SERVINGS

This recipe takes a little effort, but the results are more than worth it.
I make a tin of these every Sunday night and I pop them out when I need a
quick, handheld breakfast to go. They also make a beautiful
presentation on a plate at brunch.

1   Adjust an oven rack to the middle position and preheat the oven to 400°F. Line a rimmed baking sheet with a silicone baking mat or parchment paper.

2   Lay the strips of bacon in a single layer on a cutting board and cut them in half crosswise to yield 24 short strips.

3   Working with four short slices at a time, weave them together, overlapping like a basket. Lay each of the bacon weaves on the prepared baking sheet—you should have six in total.

4   Cover the bacon with a sheet of parchment paper and cover with a second rimmed baking sheet; this will prevent the bacon from curling during cooking.

5   Bake for 20 minutes, until almost crispy but still pliable.

6   Carefully remove the baking sheets from the oven and tip a corner over a heatproof bowl to catch the bacon drippings.

7   Brush six muffin cups with the bacon drippings. When the bacon weaves are still warm but cool enough to handle, transfer them one at a time with a metal spatula from the sheet pan into a prepared muffin cup. Press each weave down to fully line the muffin cup.

8   Divide the tomatoes between the cups. Spoon 1 teaspoon each of the avocado crema and tomatillo salsa over the tomatoes. Crack one egg into each cup and season with salt and pepper.

9   Bake for 20 minutes, or until the eggs are set.

10 Transfer the muffin tin to a wire cooling rack and allow to cool slightly. Using a sharp paring knife, gently cut around the edges of the bacon and pop out the baskets. Serve immediately.

12 strips uncured thick-cut bacon
½ cup cherry tomatoes, quartered
2 tablespoons Avocado Crema (page 31)
2 tablespoons Roasted Tomatillo Salsa (page 27)
6 large eggs
Salt and freshly ground black pepper

Get creative. This is a great way to economize on all the herb trimmings and meat scraps you have accumulated all week. Set aside a few containers that you can keep adding odds and ends to, so at the end of the week you will have essentially a "free" filling for your baskets.

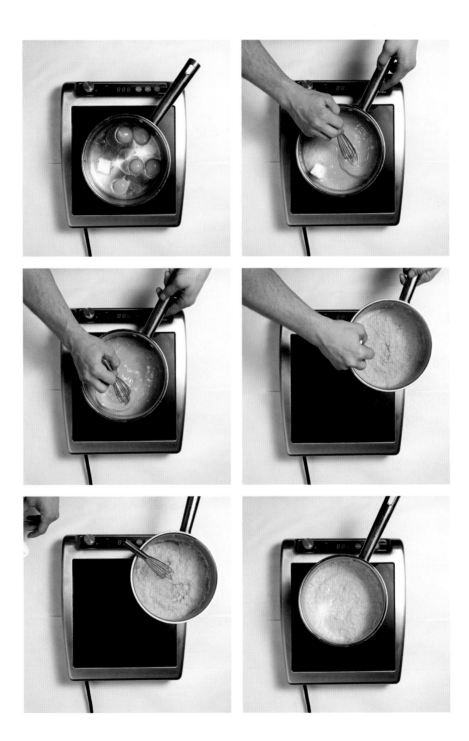

Creamy Scrambled Eggs
with Smoked Salmon and Herbs

YIELD: 1 OR 2 SERVINGS

Whenever I go camping, this is my go-to breakfast for all my friends. You can scale this recipe up to feed a large group, or keep it as is and feed yourself and maybe one other, depending on how hungry you are. After you make these once, you will be hard pressed to go back to the boring, dry scrambled eggs of your past.

5 large eggs

1½ tablespoons unsalted butter

2 tablespoons Greek yogurt

Fresh dill, chives, or scallion, finely chopped

Salt

2 ounces smoked salmon, thinly sliced

Try to find the highest-quality eggs you can. The better the source, the better for your body.

1   Crack the eggs into a small, cold saucepan. Add the butter.

2   Set the pan over medium heat and gently start whisking and breaking up the eggs. Keep whisking until you start to see steam rise from the pan, then remove the pan from the heat and continue to whisk for 10 seconds.

3   Return the pan to the heat and continue whisking; you'll see curds starting to form. Repeat this on-and-off-the-heat process a few more times, until the mixture starts to take on a thick puddinglike texture.

4   When done, remove the pan from the heat for the last time and stir in the yogurt and herbs. Season to taste with salt.

5   Transfer the eggs to one or two bowls and top with the salmon and an extra pinch of herbs. Enjoy immediately.

Start a lunch club at your workplace or in your neighborhood to get people cooking and talking.

Chapter 5

Food for Fitness and Lunches on the Go: *The Best Revenge Is Looking Good*

When I was living on a tour bus, it was all too easy to fall into the trap of delicious but terrible-for-you convenience foods (hello, Waffle House!)—which only led to feelings of lethargy and bad moods, exactly what you don't want when you're gearing up for a big performance. In an effort to eat more healthfully on the road, I got creative and came up with easy, on-the-go foods to tote along to keep me energized all day long, such as my Fattoush Salad with Pulled Chicken in a jar. It's the difference between knowing you have a healthful homemade snack within your reach and succumbing to vending machine chips and pouring another Venti Latte down your throat.

As a professional dancer, I've always known how to keep my body running at an athlete's level. No matter what your job is, sleeping well and exercising regularly is good therapy. The endorphin boost from working out stays with you all day and produces a euphoric state in the brain that actually lessens physical and mental pain (and it will make you look hot, just in case you run into a certain someone at a black-tie event).

Keep yourself in peak physical condition if you want to get what you want out of life! That includes working out regularly, eating food that gets you ready to work out, and postworkout foods that help speed recovery so you can do it all over again the next day! I am a creature of habit, and to make sure those habits stay good ones, I keep myself on a very strict routine. I have to do something physically challenging and eat well every day with very few exceptions. When I formed my routine, I became more centered and focused. The routine became the "me" time I needed and deserve. I don't have to fit it "into" my life—it *is* my life. If that means waking up earlier to get in a workout and not watching the late shows in order to be fresher for work, so be it. My therapist used to tell me, "Being an adult means deferring gratification." By deferring your gratification, you end up way more gratified once that time comes to enjoy yourself.

Raw Kale and Mint Salad
with Vegan Parmesan Vinaigrette

YIELD: 4 TO 6 SERVINGS

SALAD:
- ⅓ cup olive oil
- ½ cup whole-wheat panko bread crumbs (optional)
- Salt
- 2 bunches lacinato kale, stemmed, leaves sliced into ¼-inch-thick ribbons
- 1 cup fresh mint leaves, roughly torn by hand
- 1 serrano chile, thinly sliced
- Freshly ground black pepper

VEGAN LEMON PARMESAN VINAIGRETTE:
- ¼ cup freshly squeezed lemon juice
- 2 tablespoons nutritional yeast
- 1 tablespoon Dijon mustard
- ⅔ cup extra-virgin olive oil
- Salt and freshly ground black pepper

For the salad:

1. Line a plate with a layer of paper towels. Heat the oil in a small skillet over medium heat until shimmering. Add the panko, if using, and stir to coat in the oil. Fry until golden brown, 2 to 3 minutes, and season with a good pinch of salt. Transfer the crumbs to the prepared plate with a slotted spatula.

2. In a large bowl, toss together the kale, mint, chile, and half of the panko. Add enough dressing to coat well but not drown, tossing to coat evenly. Let stand at room temperature for 15 minutes. Finish with a sprinkle of extra panko and a few grinds of pepper.

For the Vegan Lemon Parmesan Vinaigrette: In a small bowl, whisk together the lemon juice, nutritional yeast, and mustard. Whisk in the oil and adjust the seasoning with salt and pepper. You can also place all the vinaigrette ingredients in a jam jar, cover tightly with a lid, and shake to combine. Whisk or shake the vinaigrette to reincorporate right before using.

If you are fine with dairy, sub out the nutritional yeast flakes for ¼ cup of finely grated Parmesan cheese.

Shaved Brussels and Apple Salad
with Maple, Walnuts, and Dijon

YIELD: 4 TO 6 SERVINGS

This is more of a slaw than a traditional salad, and the apples and walnuts conjure up cider mill memories from my childhood. This is one of the few salads that actually gets better as it stands. If you happen to make this for dinner one night and have leftovers, you are looking at a pretty awesome lunch to take to work the next day. Eat it by itself or top it with some shredded spatchcocked chicken (page 142).

1 In a medium-size bowl, whisk together the mustard, maple syrup, and vinegar. Whisk in the walnut oil.

2 In a large bowl, toss together the sprouts and apples—reserving some apple slices for serving—and dress with the Dijon dressing. Allow it to sit at room temperature for at least 15 minutes before serving.

3 Meanwhile, toast the walnuts in a dry skillet over medium heat until golden brown, about 5 minutes. Remove from the heat.

4 Serve on a large platter and garnish with the toasted walnuts and reserved apple slices.

- 1 tablespoon Dijon or whole-grain French mustard
- 2 tablespoons pure maple syrup
- ¼ cup cider vinegar
- ½ cup walnut oil
- 1 pound Brussels sprouts, finely sliced or shaved on a mandoline
- 2 red apples (I love Pink Lady), cored and sliced into thin half-moons, divided
- ½ cup walnuts

This salad is sturdy enough to be dressed the night before and taken to work as a stand-alone, nutritionally dense lunch.

Greens and *Grains*

YIELD: 1 SERVING

I love finding creative ways to economize my leftovers. This is a delicious money- and time-saving technique, and putting a fried egg on anything never hurt anybody. I swapped the traditional basil and pine nuts with kale and walnuts to really amp up the nutritional punch of this pesto.

KALE WALNUT PESTO
YIELD: ABOUT 2 CUPS

- **1 cup raw walnuts**
- **1 bunch curly or lacinato kale, stemmed and chopped (about 4 cups)**
- **1 cup (2 ounces) finely grated Parmesan cheese**
- **¾ cup extra-virgin olive oil**
- **½ teaspoon salt**

FOR ASSEMBLY:

- **1 tablespoon olive oil**
- **1 large egg**
- **Salt**
- **1 cup Duck Fried Rice, prepared without the duck (page 64), warmed**
- **½ cup arugula**
- **Freshly ground black pepper**
- **1 lemon**

For the kale walnut pesto: Toast the walnuts in a small skillet over medium heat until golden brown and fragrant, about 5 minutes. Transfer the nuts to a food processor and add the kale, Parmesan, oil, and salt. Process until the ingredients turn into a smooth paste. Use immediately or store in an airtight container for up to 5 days in the fridge. Alternatively, you can freeze the leftovers in an ice cube tray (see page 23 for instructions and more storage ideas).

To assemble:

1 Heat the oil in a small, nonstick skillet over medium heat until shimmering. Crack the egg into the pan, season with salt, and cook until the whites are set and the yolk has firmed to your liking. Remove from the heat.

2 Stir 1 tablespoon of the pesto into the rice and place in a serving bowl. Scatter the arugula over the rice and top it with the fried egg. Season with salt and pepper and a squeeze of lemon and enjoy immediately.

How To:
Baked Spaghetti Squash

YIELD: ABOUT 5 CUPS, DEPENDING ON THE SIZE OF YOUR SQUASH

I will always love pasta, but of all the "noodle" variations, this is one of my absolute favorites. You get the feel of noodles with way less carbs and more dietary fiber. The key is not overcooking the squash, so that you have a nice al dente texture to the finished product.

1   Adjust an oven rack to the middle position and preheat the oven to 400°F. Set a wire rack inside a rimmed baking sheet.

2   Using a sharp chef's knife, cut the squash in half lengthwise. Face the stem away from you, holding the top of the squash secure. Place the tip of your knife in the center of the squash, and like a lever, press your knife to the board. The squash has a tough exterior, so be sure your cutting board is stabilized with a rubber grip mat or a damp kitchen towel to keep it from sliding.

3   Scrape out and discard the seeds and membranes.

4   Rub the insides of the spaghetti squash with olive oil and season with salt and pepper. Wrap the halves separately in aluminum foil, making sure they are completely covered. Arrange the squash halves, cut side down, on the prepared wire rack and bake until the squash gives easily when pressed from the top and sides, about 40 minutes.

5   Carefully unwrap the squash and allow the steam to escape. Let cool slightly.

6   Using a fork, gently scrape away the flesh of the squash, which will look exactly like spaghetti. I like to do this on a large plate, making sure to spread out the squash so that it doesn't continue to steam and turn to mush.

**1 large spaghetti squash,
   scrubbed
Olive oil
Salt and freshly ground black
   pepper**

Toss with the Pumpkin Seed Pesto (page 118) or the Wild Boar Ragu (page 47). You can also use this squash instead of the miracle noodles in the Paleo Pad Thai (page 73).

Pumpkin Seed Pesto

YIELD: ABOUT 1½ CUPS PESTO

1 Place everything, except the oil, in a food processor and turn on the machine, then slowly drizzle in the oil until a thick paste forms.

2 Use or freeze within 5 days.

¾ cup fried pepitas (pumpkin seeds), strained of the oil
1 cup fresh cilantro
½ cup grated Parmesan cheese
7 tablespoons olive oil

Instead of the olive oil, substitute the reserved oil from frying the pepitas for the Winter Squash and Eggplant Gratin (page 181).

Lentil Soup

YIELD: 6 SERVINGS

This is a perfect soul-warming soup for a cold winter's day. If I am ever feeling a little bit under the weather, I make a batch of this soup, plant myself on the couch and binge-watch my Netflix, and all is right in the world.

Olive oil

2 carrots, peeled and thinly sliced (1 cup)

3 celery stalks, finely diced (1 cup)

1 yellow onion, finely diced (1 cup)

1 garlic clove, grated

1 teaspoon ground coriander

1 teaspoon ground cumin

1 teaspoon smoked pimentón or smoked paprika

Salt and freshly ground black pepper

1 cup diced canned tomatoes

2 quarts homemade or low-sodium chicken or vegetable stock

1 pound French lentils, rinsed

1 bay leaf

1 Heat 2 tablespoons of olive oil over medium-high heat in a Dutch oven or other large, heavy-bottomed pot until shimmering. Add the carrots, celery, and onion and cook until the vegetables are tender and the onion is translucent, 5 to 7 minutes. Stir in the garlic, coriander, cumin, and pimentón and cook until fragrant, about 1 minute. Season with salt and pepper.

2 Stir in the tomatoes, stock, lentils, and bay leaf and bring to a boil. Lower the heat to medium-low and simmer, covered, for 40 to 45 minutes, or until the lentils are tender. Adjust the seasonings and serve immediately.

I love to strain out some of the lentils and use them as a side dish to accompany my Slow-Baked Salmon (page 150).

Paleo
Protein Balls

YIELD: ABOUT A DOZEN BALLS

I came up with this recipe when I was training for my first CrossFit open.
I wanted something that wouldn't weigh me down yet had enough energy and
substance to keep me going through the intense workouts. I was
tempted to make this a bar, but the ball won out because it was much easier to
dip in chocolate and made for a very transportable burst of energy.

1 Place the date paste, protein powder, cherries, blueberries, hemp seeds, pecans, coconut flour, and almond butter in a food processor and process until smooth, scraping the bottom and the sides of the bowl with a rubber spatula as needed.

2 Line a baking sheet with parchment paper. Using a large spoon or a small ice cream scoop, scoop out the mixture, roll into golfball–size rounds, and set on the prepared baking sheet.

3 Fill a saucepan about a third full with water and bring to a simmer over medium heat. Place a large heatproof bowl on top—the bottom of the bowl shouldn't make contact with the water. Tip the chips into the bowl and stir constantly until they're completely melted. Remove the bowl from the heat.

4 Dip the chocolate balls in the chocolate and roll them in the coconut flakes, if using. Set them on the prepared baking sheet and place them in the freezer until firm.

½ cup Date Paste (page 37)
⅔ cup vanilla protein powder
⅓ cup frozen sour cherries
⅓ cup frozen blueberries
⅓ cup hemp seeds
⅓ cup pecans, chopped
3 tablespoons coconut flour
2 tablespoons Homemade Almond Butter (page 32)
1 cup dark chocolate chips, such as Enjoy Life brand
1 cup unsweetened coconut flakes

Tuna Snack

YIELD: 4 SERVINGS

If you walk into my house right now, you will find a jar of this tucked away in my fridge. I've never made it the same way twice, and every time I whip up a batch my wife, Sarah, insists, "This is my favorite one yet." I finally wrote it down and now you can use it as a guide to making endless variations of a classic snack.

2 (8-ounce) jars Italian tuna (spring for the good stuff)

½ cup Avocado Oil Mayo (page 34)

3 tablespoons pistachios, chopped

3 tablespoons Marcona almonds, chopped

2 tablespoons Dijon mustard

2 tablespoons pickle juice

½ Granny Smith apple, cored and diced

3 tablespoons dried cherries

1 celery stalk, finely diced

2 small pickles, finely diced

Salt and freshly ground black pepper

5 dashes of hot sauce

2 teaspoons ground turmeric

2 tablespoons chopped fresh parsley

1 Stir everything together in a large bowl, making sure to fully incorporate all the ingredients.

2 Keeps for 3 days in the fridge.

Enjoy with rye crisps, celery, or cucumber logs, if watching your carbs.

Duck Fat
Sweet Potato Chips

YIELD: ABOUT 3 CUPS CHIPS

Duck fat makes everything better, especially potatoes. Whenever I make a batch of these, the house is filled with an intoxicating aroma of the unctuous duck fat. This is one of my favorite snacks to crunch on whenever I want to kick back and watch a movie or tune in to the big game.

1 Adjust two oven racks to the upper middle and lower middle positions and preheat the oven to 250°F. Line two rimmed baking sheets with silicone baking mats or parchment paper.

2 Using a mandoline or very sharp chef's knife, slice the sweet potatoes into ⅛-inch-thick slices.

3 In a large bowl, toss the sweet potato slices in the duck fat, rubbing with your fingertips to coat.

4 Arrange the slices on the prepared baking sheets (they will shrink while they cook, so they can be very close to each other). Bake for 90 minutes, alternating the baking sheets and flipping the slices halfway through cooking.

5 Transfer the baking sheets to cooling racks and sprinkle with a pinch of salt or malt vinegar salt, if using.

2 medium-size sweet potatoes (about 6 ounces each), scrubbed and peeled
1 tablespoon duck fat, melted
Salt
Malt vinegar salt (optional)

These are great with
some malt vinegar salt
sprinkled on top.
You can also use olive oil if you
want to make this recipe vegan
or gluten free.

Fattoush Salad with Pulled Chicken

YIELD: 2 SERVINGS

I love Middle Eastern food.
When I was growing up in Dearborn, Michigan, I never knew
how lucky I was to be exposed to so many incredible cultures and cuisines
within the Arab world. My family was always perplexed by my
penchant for kebabs and my constant quest for the perfect falafel.
The bold spices always spoke to me: za'atar, ras el hanout,
and one of my go-to secret ingredients—sumac. This bold, citrusy spice is a
favorite of mine on everything from grilled or roasted meats to hummus
and, my personal favorite, fattoush salad. Fried, grilled, or raw, this
humble salad is always made with bread and whatever fresh vegetables
you have lying around.

DRESSING:

- ¼ cup freshly squeezed lemon juice
- 1 tablespoon pomegranate molasses
- 2 teaspoons sumac, plus more for finishing the salad
- 1 teaspoon champagne vinegar
- 1 teaspoon dried mint
- ½ garlic clove, minced
- ⅓ cup extra-virgin olive oil

SALAD:

- 3 tablespoons extra-virgin olive oil
- 2 (6-inch) whole-wheat pitas, ripped into 1-inch rough chunks
- ½ cup slivered or sliced almonds
- Salt
- 6 cherry tomatoes, halved
- 1 Persian cucumber, sliced into thin rounds

- 1 yellow bell pepper, cored, seeded, and thinly sliced
- ½ spatchcocked chicken (see How To, page 142), shredded
- 3 cups romaine lettuce leaves, or any combination of sturdy lettuces torn into bite-size pieces
- 1 cup fresh parsley leaves
- ½ cup fresh mint leaves
- 1 scallion, thinly sliced

Continued . . .

For the dressing: In a small bowl, whisk together the lemon juice, pomegranate molasses, sumac, champagne vinegar, dried mint, and garlic until combined. Slowly whisk in the oil until well combined; set aside.

For the salad:

1   Line a large plate with two layers of paper towels. Heat the oil in a large skillet over medium heat until shimmering. Add the pita and almonds and cook, stirring occasionally, for about 5 minutes, or until the pita is crisp and the almonds are golden. Using a slotted spoon or spatula, transfer to the prepared plate and season with salt.

2   Allow the chips to cool slightly, then transfer them a large bowl, drizzle with half of the dressing, and toss to evenly coat.

3   Add the tomatoes, cucumber, bell pepper, and chicken, tossing to coat in the dressing. Add the greens and parsley, mint, scallion, and more of the dressing, to taste, tossing to coat everything evenly. (I like to use my hands for this because it really gets a nice even coating on everything.)

4   Transfer to a large serving platter and dust the top with sumac and a good pinch of salt. Serve.

Herbed
Barley Salad

YIELD: 3 CUPS SALAD

A version of this salad graces my dinner table almost nightly in the summer months when fresh produce is abundant. I like to play around, swapping in new vegetables as they come into season, and I encourage you to do the same. There isn't much need for added seasoning or dressings, since this hearty salad is already loaded with tons of nutrients and big flavors.

2½ cups low-sodium chicken stock, or vegetable stock to make it completely vegetarian

1 cup uncooked pearl barley

Salt

1 medium-size English cucumber, peeled, seeded, and diced

1 tomato, quartered, seeded and diced

¼ cup loosely packed fresh mint leaves, roughly chopped

¼ cup fresh flat-leaf parsley, roughly chopped

2 scallions, finely sliced

4 ounces feta cheese, coarsely crumbled

Extra-virgin olive oil, as needed

Juice of 1 lemon

Freshly ground black pepper

1 Bring the stock to a boil in a medium-size saucepan over high heat. Stir in the barley and ½ teaspoon of salt, cover and reduce the heat to low. Cook until all the water has been absorbed and the barley is tender, about 45 minutes. Remove from the heat, fluff the barley with a fork, and transfer to a large bowl. Allow the barley to cool completely.

2 Stir in the cucumber, tomato, mint, parsley, and scallions. Gently stir in the feta. Drizzle with olive oil and lemon juice, season to taste with salt and pepper, and serve.

> Barley is low on the glycemic index, so it won't spike your blood sugar like other refined grains and it's loaded with fiber. The soluble fiber contained in barley helps prevent the cholesterol in the foods you eat from being absorbed into your bloodstream.
> The salad is sturdy enough to survive overnight, but any longer than that will compromise the flavor and texture. You can also use the Microwave Veggies (page 136) when tomatoes aren't in season.

Experiment with any seasoning you may have on hand; just remember to season lightly here because as the kale cooks it will lose its moisture and intensify the flavors.

Harissa-Spiced
Kale Chips

YIELD: 3 TO 4 CUPS CHIPS

These make a wonderful crunchy snack
that won't leave you starving for your next meal.

2 bunches kale, stemmed
1 tablespoon olive oil
½ teaspoon kosher salt
½ teaspoon dried harissa spice

1 Preheat the oven to 275°F.

2 Wash and dry the kale thoroughly.

3 Place in a large bowl and drizzle the oil on top, mixing with your hands to coat evenly.

4 Arrange the kale leaves flat on two sheet pans covered with parchment or a silicone baking mat. Lightly season with the salt and harissa.

5 Bake until the leaves are crisp and opaque, 20 to 25 minutes.

If you don't happen to have rubber gloves lying around the house, I use a small, resealable plastic bag to hold the beet and then peel away the skin with a paper towel. If the beets are properly roasted, the skin should slip off very easily.

Roasted Beet Salad
with Lemon, Ginger, and Balsamic

YIELD: 2 SERVINGS

This salad makes a perfect dinner and actually gets better
the next day when you pack your lunch for work. Skip the salad bar at your local
grocery store and turn your leftovers into lunch.

LEMON-GINGER OIL:
YIELD: ABOUT ½ CUP
- **½ cup olive oil**
- **1 (2-inch piece) fresh ginger, grated (1 tablespoon)**
- **2 teaspoons finely grated lemon zest**
- **1 teaspoon salt**

BEETS:
- **4 red beets, scrubbed and dried**
- **Olive oil**
- **Salt and freshly ground black pepper**

TO SERVE:
- **½ cup labne or Greek yogurt**
- **¼ cup blanched hazelnuts, toasted and chopped**
- **Maldon or other sea salt**
- **Freshly ground black pepper**
- **1 tablespoon Balsamic Glaze (recipe follows)**
- **3 tablespoons fresh dill fronds, for garnish**

For the lemon-ginger oil: Combine all the ingredients in a small saucepan. Heat over medium heat to just below a simmer, then remove from the heat. Carefully pour the oil into a blender and blend until smooth. Use immediately, or store in an airtight container in the fridge for up to 3 days.

For the beets:

1 Adjust an oven rack to the middle position and preheat the oven to 400°F.

2 Trim off the tops of the beets, snip off and discard part of the long bottom root, quarter, and place in a large bowl. If the beet greens look good, reserve them for salads or juices.

3 Add about 3 tablespoons of olive oil to the beets; they should be coated. Season them with salt and pepper and place them, cut side up, on a baking sheet. Cover loosely with aluminum foil and roast for 35 to 45 minutes, or until the beets are easily pierced with a knife. Transfer the baking sheet to a cooling rack, and when cool enough to handle, peel them, using a paper towel.

To serve: Spoon the labne into an even layer on a large plate. Arrange the warm beets on top and sprinkle with the hazelnuts. Season with a pinch of Maldon salt, drizzle with the 1 tablespoon of the lemon-ginger oil and the balsamic glaze. Finish with the dill.

Balsamic Glaze

YIELD: ABOUT ¼ CUP

- **½ cup balsamic vinegar**
- **1 tablespoon pure maple syrup**

Whisk together the two ingredients and pour them into a small saucepan set over medium-high heat. Reduce the mixture until it is thick and syrupy, about 5 minutes.

Sugar Snap Pea and Radish Salad
with Roasted Sesame Ponzu

YIELD: 2 SERVINGS

This is a bowl of spring and my take on a Japanese pub classic. The roasted sesame is a nice contrast to the citrusy ponzu. I really love the Joyva brand of tahini paste. It's one of the few that uses roasted sesame seeds and it's readily available at most markets.

1 Prepare a large bowl with equal parts ice and water and set aside.

2 Bring a large pot of water to boil, add the sugar snap peas, and cook for 1 minute. Transfer the snaps from the water directly into the ice bath to stop the cooking.

3 After 3 minutes, remove the snaps from the water and drain on a paper towel.

4 Using a very sharp knife, slice them lengthwise into thin, long ribbons.

5 Toss the snaps and almost all the radish (reserving some for garnish) in the roasted sesame ponzu sauce, about 2 tablespoons at a time, until evenly coated but not swimming in the dressing.

6 Top with the reserved radish slices, sesame seeds, a drizzle of oil, pinch of salt, and a squeeze of lemon.

½ pound snap peas, strings removed
1 radish, thinly sliced
Roasted Sesame Ponzu Sauce (recipe follows)
Sesame seeds
Toasted sesame oil
Maldon salt
Lemon

Roasted Sesame Ponzu Sauce

YIELD: ABOUT ½ CUP

Place everything in a food processor or blender and blend until smooth.

¼ cup roasted sesame paste (I love Joyva)
3 tablespoons plus 2 teaspoons ponzu sauce
4 tablespoons water

Store-bought sesame paste tends to separate as it sits on the shelf. I always scrape it out of the can into a food processor and recombine the mixture. Rinse out the can and pour the smooth paste back, seal, and keep in the fridge.

Microwave
Veggies

YIELD: 2 CUPS VEGGIES

This is the easiest, fastest, and—contrary to what most people think—most nutritious way to cook veggies. The short cooking time and lack of nutrient-leaching water keep these veggies full of color and result in an incredible texture. You can bring one of your homemade sauces with you to work and have a gourmet meal at your office.

1 Place the veggies in a microwave-safe bowl and cover tightly with plastic wrap.

2 Microwave on HIGH for 2½ to 3 minutes. Remove the bowl from the microwave and poke holes in the plastic to release the steam, then remove the plastic. Season as you like and enjoy.

2 cups mixed seasonal vegetables, cleaned and cut into ½-inch pieces

I love these tossed in the kale pesto over Duck Fried Rice (page 64) or added to the Herbed Barley Salad (page 129) when summer veggies aren't an option.

Goji Berry and Dark Chocolate *Energy Mix*

YIELD: 2¾ CUPS MIX

If you happen to bump into me on the street, I am guaranteed to have a batch of this on me. The combination of healthy fats and protein keeps me fueled up when I need a snack between meals.

1 cup raw macadamia nuts
¾ cup raw pepitas (pumpkin seeds)
½ cup goji berries
½ cup dark chocolate chips

1 Toss all the ingredients together in a medium-size bowl and enjoy.

2 The mix can be stored in an airtight container for up to 3 weeks at room temperature.

Goji berries are one of my favorite superfoods. They are delicious and loaded with antioxidants. Enjoy Life brand makes a great vegan chocolate chip, if you want to make this recipe vegan or Paleo.

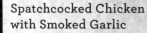
Spatchcocked Chicken
with Smoked Garlic

Chapter 6

One-Dish Wonders: *Dinner in a Flash*

Life doesn't wait. Commitments with family, friends, job, gym, and all of your other responsibilities are constantly crowding your calendar … and yes, you have to eat, too. Even if you're lucky enough to live with a natural-born cook, you still have to hold up your end sometimes—and dinners out/take-out can get a little tiring (and a lot fattening) and leave you feeling unfulfilled and empty after an exhausting day. So, let's get focused and get the party started. Why suffer through another plateful of limp French fries when you can have a homemade feast on a Tuesday and make your mouth water on a Wednesday!? Even when you've been on your feet or on your ass all day, cooking your own meals can be an extremely gratifying experience.

The other night, I was home alone and the cupboard was, if not bare, definitely not overflowing. I found a box of farfalle and a jar of tuna in the pantry, some frozen peas in the freezer, a few floating capers, and a lemon—and in the time that it took me to boil water, I was able to pull together a fair replica of Tonno al Limone: tuna with lemon. In five minutes. Because I know that good food doesn't take a long time, just some creative energy. Some people look at dinner as a collection of mains and sides. I look at it as a complete dish, all in one, all of the flavors together.

My approach to midweek dining is one-dish dining. There's no need to fuss with mains and sides and make four separate dishes or multiple courses. Top a salad with protein; add vegetables to your entrée, and you've got a streamlined dinner that is fully nutritious and completely delicious. And if you've prepped, you can feast midweek with even less effort. I don't need my food in five separate bowls...I don't need the tuna on the side...

Just remember that food should taste crisp and fresh, and it doesn't need to be swimming in a complicated dressing or sauce. A squeeze of fresh lemon and a drizzle of oil goes a long way to elevate a dish to a whole other level. That's what these recipes are: ways to make basic ingredients taste *amazing*, in less time, with less effort—and with more enjoyment. When you start with quality pantry goods and beautiful seasonal ingredients, your only job as the chef is not to screw them up.

PREP KITCHEN:
Experts prep days in advance, and so should you. Setting aside a prep day (really only an hour or so on a day off) is critical to having the ability to whip up a true 20-minute or even 10-minute meal loaded with protein, complex carbs, and even a healthful treat. Carry your own lunch and make your own dinner—in the long run, it will be a lot easier on your waistline and your wallet!

Skirt Steak with Chimichurri Sauce

YIELD: 2 OR 3 PORTIONS

I love this meal because it's full of fresh herbaceous flavors
and really comes together in a flash. It's okay to use less-expensive olive
oil to cook with and save your fancy olive oils for making
sauces or dressings that will finish a dish.

STEAK:
- **1 pound skirt steak**
- **Salt and freshly ground black pepper**
- **Olive oil**

CHIMICHURRI SAUCE:
- **¾ cup fresh parsley, chopped**
- **½ cup fresh cilantro, chopped**
- **2 tablespoons fresh oregano, chopped**
- **½ small roasted red pepper, chopped (about 1 tablespoon)**
- **1 to 2 garlic cloves, finely minced or grated on a Microplane**
- **Finely grated zest of ½ lemon**
- **¼ cup freshly squeezed lemon juice**
- **1 teaspoon red wine vinegar**
- **½ teaspoon red pepper flakes**
- **½ teaspoon salt**
- **⅔ cup olive oil**

For the steak: Allow the steak to sit out at room temperature for 30 minutes prior to cooking.

For the chimichurri sauce:

1. Meanwhile, combine the parsley, cilantro, oregano, red pepper, garlic, lemon zest, lemon juice, vinegar, red pepper flakes, and salt in a medium-size bowl. Whisk in the olive oil and allow to sit at room temperature.

2. Heat a grill or grill pan over high heat until beginning to smoke.

3. Season the steak well with salt and black pepper.

4. Drizzle the steak with just enough olive oil to cover and place on the hot grill. Cook for 4 minutes per side for medium rare. Transfer the steak to a cutting board and allow to rest for 5 to 10 minutes prior to serving.

5. Serve with the chimichurri.

This recipe works really well as a marinade for chicken.

How To:
Spatchcocked Chicken
with Smoked Garlic

YIELD: 1 CHICKEN

This is my go-to when I want a roasted chicken but don't want to wait hours for it to be done. The intense heat gets the skin as crisp as a potato chip. I make one of these at the beginning of each week and then parse it out into multiple recipes.

SMOKED GARLIC PASTE:
6 garlic cloves, minced to a paste
1½ teaspoons smoked hot Spanish paprika
¾ teaspoon salt
Olive oil

CHICKEN:
1 (3½-pound) whole chicken
Salt and freshly ground black pepper
Olive oil

For the smoked garlic paste: In a small bowl, mix together the garlic, paprika, and salt. Add just enough olive oil to make a paste. Set aside while you spatchcock the chicken.

For the chicken:

1   Adjust an oven rack to the middle position and preheat the oven to 450°F. Set a wire rack inside a rimmed baking sheet.

2   Bring the chicken out of the fridge 30 minutes before cooking. Lay the chicken on a clean, stabilized cutting board, breast side down.

3   Using very sharp kitchen shears, cut along the side of the spine, from the tail end to the neck. Repeat on other side. Reserve the backbone for stock.

4 Using a very sharp knife, score vertically down the breastbone, then flip the bird over, breast side up. Press down firmly with the palm of your hand until you hear a "pop" and the chicken is lying flat. Tuck the wings under the breast.

5 Use your fingers to carefully loosen the skin away from the meat. Spread the smoked garlic paste under the skin, covering the breast and thigh meat.

6 Season both sides of the chicken generously with salt and pepper. Set the chicken, breast side up, on the prepared baking sheet. Drizzle with olive oil and rub to evenly coat the skin. Roast for 40 to 45 minutes, or until the thigh juices run clear when pierced with a knife. Transfer the baking sheet to a cooling rack and allow to rest for 10 minutes prior to carving.

Pork Tenderloin
with 5-Minute Cherry Applesauce

YIELD: 4 SERVINGS

A pork roast is one of the most enjoyable culinary delights. Usually, a large group gathers and waits hours for a perfectly cooked piece of meat to emerge from the oven to be relished by all. The fumes are intoxicating and everyone is seated around the beautifully set table. I hate to shatter the Norman Rockwell picture that I'm painting here, but it's a weeknight, you just got home from work—and nobody has time for all that. You need to eat now!
This ain't your grandma's dry Sunday roast; this is a restaurant-quality dish on your table in minutes.

For the pork:

1. Adjust an oven rack to the middle position and preheat the oven to 400°F. Set a wire rack inside a rimmed baking sheet.

2. Heat a grill pan over medium-high heat.

3. Cut the pork loin in half, and season the halves liberally with salt and pepper. Rub a generous amount of olive oil all over the pork and sprinkle with the rosemary and oregano.

4. Cook the pork for about 3 minutes per side, or until nicely seared. Transfer the pork to the prepared rack and roast for 10 to 12 minutes more, for a beautiful rosy pink center.

5. Transfer the baking sheet to a cooling rack and allow the pork to rest for 5 minutes.

PORK:
- **1 (1½-pound) pork tenderloin, trimmed of any silver skin or sinew**
- **Salt and freshly ground black pepper**
- **Extra-virgin olive oil**
- **Leaves from 1 rosemary sprig, minced (1 tablespoon)**
- **2 tablespoons dried oregano**

CHERRY APPLESAUCE:
- **3 Granny Smith apples, peeled, cored, and thinly sliced**
- **¼ cup cherry preserves**

For the cherry applesauce: While the pork is resting, place the apples in a microwave-safe bowl and wrap it tightly with plastic wrap. Cook for 2 minutes 15 seconds on HIGH. Carefully remove the bowl from the microwave and poke holes in the plastic wrap to release the steam. If the apples aren't completely soft, rewrap the bowl and microwave them for a few seconds longer. Transfer the apples to a blender, add the cherry preserves, and blend on high speed until smooth, scraping down the bottom and sides as needed.

To serve: Cut the pork into ½-inch slices and serve with a generous amount of cherry applesauce on the side.

> Your experience with the microwave probably doesn't extend beyond popcorn or a periodic frozen dinner, but it's actually one of the least appreciated and underutilized pieces of equipment in the kitchen. When used creatively, it becomes a timesaving workhorse in you arsenal.

Microwave-Braised *Radicchio and Marcona Almonds* with Buttermilk Dressing

YIELD: 4 SERVINGS

This is my update on that nutritionally devoid iceberg wedge that is ubiquitous on every steakhouse menu. The radicchio has a perfect balance between braised and crunchy, and it never hurts to put blue cheese on anything. You could pair this with a simply grilled piece of meat, but I've been known to eat this as a main course with a big glass of red wine.

For the buttermilk dressing: In a medium-size bowl, whisk together the Avocado Oil Mayo, buttermilk, and chives. Season with salt and pepper and set aside. The dressing can be made up to 3 days in advance and stored in an airtight container in the fridge.

For the radicchio and almonds:

1 Wash the radicchio and remove any wilted or bruised outer leaves. Cut the head lengthwise into four pieces, leaving the stem intact. Place the radicchio in a microwave-safe dish and drizzle with olive oil. Wrap the bowl tightly with plastic wrap, and microwave on HIGH for 60 seconds.

2 Remove the bowl from the microwave and poke holes in the plastic wrap to release the steam, then remove the plastic.

3 Holding your knife at an angle, cut away and discard the core portion of each quarter and divide among four plates. Dress each piece, then top with the almonds. Grate the blue cheese on top of each and serve immediately.

BUTTERMILK DRESSING:
- ½ cup **Avocado Oil Mayo (page 34)**
- ½ cup **buttermilk**
- 1 tablespoon **minced chives**
- **Salt and freshly ground black pepper**

RADICCHIO AND ALMONDS:
- 1 head **radicchio**
- **Olive oil**
- ¼ cup **Marcona almonds, chopped**
- 4 ounces **blue cheese, in one piece, frozen**

Extra blue cheese? No problem. It works well grated over a perfectly cooked filet mignon in lieu of butter. I often freeze grated Cheddar or Parmesan if I find that I have a surplus. Just make sure to clearly write a date on them and use within 6 months.

Chicken Saltimbocca

YIELD: 2 PORTIONS

2 bone-in, skin-on chicken thighs, bones removed
Salt and freshly ground black pepper
4 sage leaves
2 slices nitrate-free prosciutto
Wondra flour or potato starch (optional)
2 tablespoons olive oil
1 tablespoon unsalted butter, cut into 2 pieces
½ radicchio head, cored and broken into large leaves
2 tablespoons chopped fresh flat-leaf parsley
Juice of ½ lemon

1 Season the chicken on both sides gently with salt and pepper. Arrange two sage leaves on the flesh side of each piece of chicken, then cover each piece of chicken with a slice of prosciutto. Use a meat tenderizer to gently pound the prosciutto into the meat. Sprinkle a little Wondra on the skin side of the chicken and pat off any excess.

2 Heat the oil in a large skillet over medium-high heat until it just begins to smoke. Arrange the chicken, skin side down, in the skillet, pressing down to ensure evenly crisped skin. If you have a grill press, this would be a good time to use it; if not, a heavy iron pan works as well.

3 Cook until the skin is golden brown and crisp, about 8 minutes. Add the butter and cook for 2 minutes longer, swirling the pan to get the butter beneath the skin.

4 Flip the chicken and cook until the prosciutto is crisp, about 3 minutes longer. Transfer the chicken to a plate to rest.

5 Increase the heat to high and toss in the radicchio leaves. Cook for 5 minutes, or until nicely wilted. Remove from the heat, add the parsley and lemon juice, and toss to combine. Divide the radicchio between two plates and arrange the chicken on top. Serve.

Wondra flour is finely milled and already cooked and dried, so it won't clump if you add it straight into a hot gravy or sauce. Since it is so finely milled, it allows for the most delicate and crispy crust to any protein you sauté. If you are grain free, sub potato starch.

To remove the bones, lay the chicken thigh, skin side down, on a cutting board. Using the tip of a sharp paring knife or sturdy kitchen scissors, make an incision along the top of the bone and keep deepening the incision until the bone is visible. Slip your fingers under the bone and trim the meat as close to the bone as possible, carefully lifting the bone away.

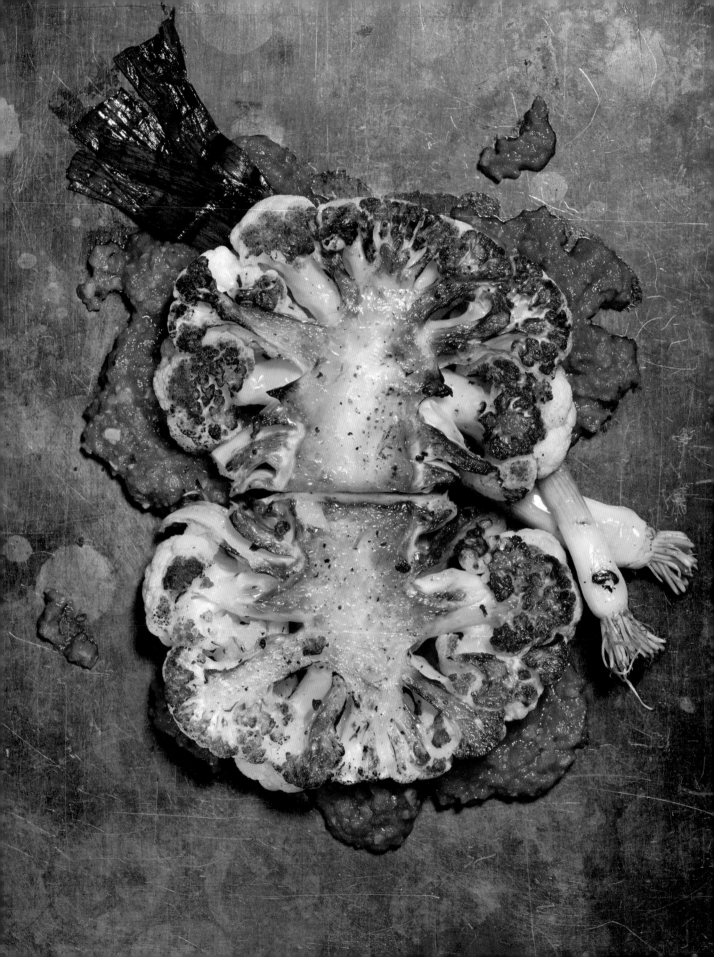

Cauliflower Steak
with Romesco Sauce and Charred Scallions

YIELD: 2 SERVINGS

This is my version of a vegetarian steak night. I love taking large cuts of vegetables and cooking them with meat-type preparations and big robust flavors. The Romesco freezes well and makes a meal out of any vegetable or meat in a flash.

Olive oil
1 (1-inch thick) slice cauliflower
Salt
3 scallions, ends trimmed
Romesco Sauce (page 25)

1 Preheat the oven to 400°F. Heat 1 tablespoon of oil in a medium-size cast-iron skillet over medium-high heat until shimmering. Add the cauliflower and season with salt. Place another pan on top to help keep the cauliflower pressed down in the pan. Cook for about 3 minutes per side, until slightly charred at the edges. Pop the pan into the oven and cook for about 8 more minutes, or until tender, flipping the steak halfway through.

2 Remove the steak from the pan and set aside. Toss the scallions in just enough olive oil to coat. Carefully set the iron skillet on the range over medium-high heat and char the scallions for about 3 minutes per side.

3 To serve, place a good amount of Romesco Sauce on a plate. Top with the scallions, then set the steak on top.

Canned plum tomatoes work in a pinch, but skip the roasting step if using them.
To prep a cauliflower "steak," simply trim off and discard the base leaves, then carefully cut the cauliflower vertically from the top to the stem into 1-inch-thick slices. Depending on the size, you can get two or three steaks from the center of the cauliflower. Reserve the remainder for a separate use, such as Cauliflower Fried Rice (page 41).

Slow-Baked Salmon
with Miso Glaze

YIELD: 2 SERVINGS

I made this dish no less than a thousand times during my time
under the great master Nobu, and I swore after I left that I'd never cook it again.
I have since caved and written my own version. Here's a simplified, healthier
version of Nobu-san's genius creation that has spurned countless imitators.
I guess you can add me to that list now as well.

For the miso glaze: In a small saucepan, whisk together the agave, miso, and mirin, if using. Bring the mixture to a boil over medium-high heat, whisking until smooth. Remove from the heat and let cool to room temperature before using. The glaze can be stored in an airtight container for up to 1 week in the fridge.

For the salmon:

1 Place the salmon in a large resealable plastic bag. Pour in the glaze, seal the bag, and let it marinate overnight in the fridge.

2 Remove the salmon from the fridge 30 minutes prior to cooking. Adjust an oven rack to the topmost position (about 6 inches away from the broiler) and a second rack to the middle position. Preheat the oven to 285°F.

3 Wipe off and reserve the excess glaze. Place the salmon fillets on a sheet pan and bake on the middle rack for 12 to 14 minutes, or just until cooked through. Turn the broiler to HIGH, lightly brush the salmon with the reserved glaze, and broil for 2 minutes.

4 Serve with the Cauliflower Fried Rice.

MISO GLAZE:
- **½ cup agave nectar**
- **½ cup white miso paste**
- **2 teaspoons mirin (optional)**

SALMON:
- **2 (6-ounce) salmon fillets, skin removed**

TO SERVE:
- **Cauliflower Fried Rice (page 41)**

The key to the success
of this dish is the low
temperature it's cooked at.

Chile-Glazed Sea Bass
with Spicy Basil Greens

YIELD: 2 SERVINGS

It always happened in the middle of a busy lunch service: I would be working on no less than 20 things, completely slammed with orders, and Jean-Georges would gracefully waltz into the kitchen holding a beautiful fillet of fish. He would lay it on my station and, in his charming way, say, "Look what a beautiful fish... When you have time, eh?" Which in my head translated to, "This is your boss and one of the greatest culinary legends of history. Move your ass and cook it now!" He would then proceed to stand at my station, pick up my knife, and leisurely start chopping kale, Swiss chard, or some other vegetable to accompany said fish. He moved with ease and elegance as if he was born with a knife in his hand. He is a master of taking simple ingredients that by themselves are not very impressive and making masterpieces. This dish is my homage to the many lunches I cooked for a legend.

2 (6-ounce) fillets of sea bass, cod, or any firm whitefish

Salt

Spicy Basil Greens (recipe follows)

SRIRACHA CHILE GLAZE:

⅓ cup honey

2 tablespoons Sriracha

1 tablespoon tamari or coconut aminos

1 tablespoon freshly squeezed lime juice

For the fish: Adjust an oven rack to the middle position and preheat the oven to 300°F. Remove the fish from the refrigerator 20 minutes prior to cooking.

For the Sriracha chile glaze:

1   Meanwhile, in a small bowl, whisk together the honey, Sriracha, tamari, and lime juice: set aside.

2   Place the fish on a rimmed baking sheet and season it lightly with salt. Brush it with a generous amount of the glaze, reserving some for serving.

Continued . . .

3 Cook for 12 to 14 minutes, or until a cake tester can be inserted without any resistance. Prepare the spicy basil greens while the fish is cooking.

4 Place a large mound of the greens on a plate and top with the fish.

5 Brush with more of the glaze and serve.

Spicy Basil Greens

YIELD: 2 SERVINGS

1 Heat the oil in a large skillet over medium heat. Once the oil starts to shimmer, add the garlic slices and cook for 1 minute, add the chopped chard stems, and cook for another minute. Toss in the spinach and serrano and cook until wilted, stirring constantly.

2 Remove from the heat, add the basil leaves, and toss to wilt

3 Season with salt and pepper.

1 tablespoon olive oil
1 garlic clove, thinly sliced
2 rainbow chard stalks, leaves removed and roughly chopped, stems reserved and diced
2 cups spinach leaves
3 thin slices serrano chili
½ cup fresh basil leaves
Salt and freshly ground black pepper

Tonno al Limone

YIELD: 4 SERVINGS

This is the ultimate pantry meal. I always have these ingredients
in my house and I know dinner is less than 10 minutes away.
I like to splurge on the Italian tuna because it is so far superior in taste
and texture, but the canned will work in a pinch.

1 pound farfalle pasta

**Finely grated zest and juice of
1 lemon**

**2 tablespoons capers, rinsed
and drained well**

1 cup frozen peas

2 (8-ounce) jars of tuna

**¼ cup fresh flat-leaf parsley,
roughly chopped**

2 tablespoons minced chives

Red pepper flakes

**Salt and freshly ground black
pepper**

1 Cook the pasta in salted water
according to package instructions and drain, reserving 1 cup
of the cooking water

2 Place the reserved pasta water,
lemon zest and juice, and
capers in a large skillet and
bring to a simmer over medium-
high heat. Add the pasta and
peas and stir to coat.

3 Stir in the tuna and its oil, gently
breaking it apart with the back
of a wooden spoon.

4 Add the parsley, chives, and a
pinch of the red pepper flakes,
stirring to combine. Add salt and
black pepper to taste. Serve.

I make a big batch of
this because it's just as
good, if not better, the
next day.

When buying scallops, look for the ones
that are dry packed and avoid those that
are covered in or near liquid.

Scallops
with Strawberry Salsa

YIELD: 2 PORTIONS

This is a healthful fresh and fast summer meal that is on your table in less than 20 minutes. Scallops have a very mild flavor, are a very lean and nutritious protein source, and make a perfect complement to the spicy and slightly sweet salsa.

2 tablespoons unsalted butter, ghee, or grapeseed oil

6 large scallops, adductor muscle removed

Strawberry Salsa (recipe follows)

Salt

3 fresh basil leaves, thinly sliced

1 Melt the butter or heat the ghee in a medium-size skillet over medium-high heat, swirling to coat the entire pan. Pat the scallops dry with a paper towel and season them with salt.

2 Place the scallops 1 inch apart around the edge of the pan, starting from the 12 o'clock position. Sear undisturbed for 3 minutes. Flip and cook for 1 more minute.

3 Transfer the scallops to a serving plate and top with the strawberry salsa and basil chiffonade.

Strawberry Salsa

YIELD: ABOUT 3 CUPS

2 plum tomatoes

2 cups hulled and diced strawberries (½-inch dice, from about 3 cups whole strawberries)

2 tablespoons Balsamic Glaze (page 133)

Juice of ½ lime

½ teaspoon seeded and finely diced serrano chile

½ teaspoon salt

2 tablespoons finely chopped fresh basil

1 Bring a medium-size pot of water to a boil and have a large bowl of ice water nearby.

2 Remove the core from the tomatoes and score the opposite end in an X pattern with the tip of a sharp knife.

3 Carefully place them in the boiling water, count to 10, and, using a slotted spoon, transfer them to the ice bath. After about 5 minutes, take out the tomatoes, and using a paring knife, carefully remove and discard the skins. Quarter the tomatoes and cut away the insides. Dice the slices into ½-inch dice.

4 Place everything in a large bowl, stir to combine, and allow to marinate for 15 minutes before serving.

Part Three:
Throw a Party

Chapter 7

Be the Best Brunch Spot in Town: *Brunch and Sides*

Whenever my little sister Allie comes over, she demands a big plate of eggs, no matter the time of day. And I'm happy to oblige, because eggs are my absolute favorite food to cook, and they're always a crowd-pleaser.

Want the highest Yelp review in your neighborhood for your breakfasts and plenty of foot traffic? Fix up a mess of these healthy, delicious recipes and sides. And remember that weekends were made to help you forget what you've had to deal with during the week and to savor time away from the desk with friends. So, get the skillet sizzling and start the cocktail sipping!

Save your cash! Have a brunch potluck with friends. Encourage everyone to bring the foods we all love: vodka, vodka, vodka, and oh yeah, tomato juice.

Applesauce and crème fraîche are amazing, but If you want to make this an over-the-top crowd-pleaser, top with some caviar or salmon roe.

Sweet Potato
Scallion Latkes

YIELD: ABOUT 12 LATKES (DEPENDING ON SIZE)

My best friend's dad taught me how to make latkes over 15 years ago and I've since been on a quest to see how many different variations I could come up with. I've used different potatoes and onions, and an array of spices. I finally landed on this mix of scallions and sweet potatoes as my absolute favorite combination. Break out the sour cream and applesauce and go to town.

1 pound sweet potatoes
1 tablespoon grass-fed butter or olive oil
1 cup diced yellow onion
½ cup potato starch
2 scallions, thinly sliced
¼ teaspoon garlic powder
½ teaspoon salt
2 large eggs, beaten
Neutral oil of your choice
Crème fraîche
Cherry Applesauce (pages 144–145)

1 Preheat the oven to 200°F and place a wire rack over a sheet pan inside.

2 Using a food processor or box grater, carefully grate the sweet potato and transfer to a large bowl.

3 Place a 10-inch skillet over medium heat. Add 1 teaspoon of the butter and heat for about 40 seconds.

4 Add the onion to the pan and cook until translucent, about 3 minutes. Remove from heat and let cool.

5 Use your hands to toss the potatoes, onion, potato starch, scallions, garlic powder, and salt until well combined.

6 Stir in the eggs.

7 Place a heavy-bottomed skillet over medium heat and pour in ¼ inch of oil.

8 Form the pancake mixture into 3-inch rounds and carefully place them in the skillet, pressing them flat with a spatula, being mindful not to overcrowd.

9 Working in batches, fry them 2 to 3 minutes per side until nicely browned and cooked through.

10 As they finish, place them on the prepared wire rack in the oven to keep warm. Serve with crème fraîche and cherry applesauce.

Spiced Muffins

YIELD: 1 DOZEN MUFFINS

Baking without grains can be quite tricky. After many trials and errors,
this was the first muffin that actually passed for the real thing. I also like to
bake it into mini loaf pans like a traditional quick bread.

1 Adjust an oven rack to the middle position and preheat the oven to 350°F. Line a 12-cup muffin tin with liners or lightly coat with baking spray.

2 Sift the coconut flour, sugar, arrowroot, tapioca flour, pumpkin spice mix, baking powder, salt, and xanthan gum into a large bowl.

3 In a medium-size bowl, beat the eggs. Whisk in the buttermilk and butter and pour into the dry ingredients. Stir well to combine. Fill the prepared muffin cups with the batter, filling each cup about two-thirds of the way full.

4 Bake for 25 to 30 minutes, until the tops are golden brown and a toothpick inserted into the center comes out clean. Transfer to a cooling rack and allow to cool slightly before removing the muffins from the tin.

Baking spray (optional)
1 cup coconut flour
¾ cup cane sugar
½ cup arrowroot powder
½ cup tapioca flour
2 tablespoons Pumpkin Spice Mix (recipe follows)
2 teaspoons baking powder
1 teaspoon salt
1 teaspoon xanthan gum
3 large eggs
1½ cups buttermilk
2½ tablespoons unsalted butter, melted

Pumpkin Spice Mix

YIELD: 3¾ TEASPOONS

¼ cup ground cinnamon
1 teaspoon ground ginger
1 teaspoon ground nutmeg
¾ teaspoon ground allspice
¾ teaspoon ground cloves

Stir the cinnamon, ginger, nutmeg, allspice, and cloves together in a small bowl. Use immediately or store in an airtight container for up to 3 months at room temperature.

To make pumpkin spice sugar, add 1 part pumpkin spice mix to 3 parts sugar and use in the Cheater Doughnuts (page 236).

Shakshouka

YIELD: 4 SERVINGS

While I was traveling around the Middle East, this was my
go-to breakfast almost every day. It has the perfect combination of onions,
spices, and energizing protein. I loved it so much I would collect
different recipes and stories from all my new friends along the way. Below is a
simplified amalgamation of many generations of cooking.

1 Heat the olive oil in a large skillet over medium heat until shimmering. Add the onion and bell pepper and cook, stirring occasionally, until they're completely soft, about 15 minutes.

2 Add the garlic, harissa, cumin, paprika, and serrano and cook until fragrant and the harissa paste has darkened, 2 minutes more.

3 Stir in the tomatoes, sugar, if using, and a good pinch of salt and black pepper.

4 Simmer until the tomatoes have reduced and thickened, 8 to 10 minutes. Spread the chard leaves over the tomato mixture and crack the eggs on top. Cover and cook until the whites are set and the yolks are set but still a little runny, about 12 minutes. Serve.

3 tablespoons olive oil

1 large yellow onion, thinly sliced

1 red bell pepper, seeds and ribs removed, thinly sliced

2 garlic cloves, thinly sliced

1 tablespoon harissa paste

2 teaspoons ground cumin

1 teaspoon sweet paprika

½ serrano chile, seeds and ribs removed, minced

1 (28-ounce) can plum tomatoes, roughly chopped, juices reserved

½ teaspoon granulated sugar (optional)

Salt and freshly ground black pepper

3 rainbow chard leaves, roughly chopped (1½ cups)

6 large eggs

Always pick a watermelon that feels heavy for its size and has a very large yellow sun spot on it. Both are indicators that the melon was left out in one place to ripen properly.

Use any leftovers for the Watermelon Chia Agua Fresca (page 89).

Melon, Basil, and
Goat Cheese Salad

YIELD: 6 SERVINGS

This makes a great summer party appetizer, or, if you're like me, you'll make a lunch out of it and devour the whole thing. The crunch and saltiness of the Maldon complements the sweet juiciness of the watermelon. Try this recipe with other types of melon and cheeses as well.

1 baby seedless watermelon, cantaloupe, or honeydew melon
6 ounces goat cheese, chilled
½ bunch basil (about 1 cup leaves)
Extra-virgin olive oil
Maldon or other flaky sea salt
Freshly ground black pepper

1 Remove the rind from the melon. Cut into logs about 1 inch thick and 4 inches long.

2 Break apart the goat cheese into rough chunks and place on top of the melon. Garnish with the basil and top with a good drizzle of olive oil, a healthy pinch of Maldon salt, and a few grinds of black pepper. Serve immediately.

Grilled Peach and *Burrata Salad*

YIELD: 4 SERVINGS

In the summer when the grill is fired up, I love tossing anything and everything on there to get that awesome charred goodness. Peaches are one of my favorites for this because they are sturdy and become otherworldly delicious after a few minutes over the coals.

1 Toss the kale with enough white balsamic vinaigrette to thoroughly coat. Allow to stand for 10 minutes.

2 Heat a grill or grill pan to high. Brush the grill clean and lightly oil. Place the peaches on the grill, cut side down, and grill about 3 minutes, turning once. If the grill grates are too wide, use a grill basket. Transfer to a plate.

3 Arrange the kale on a serving platter. Tear the burrata apart with your hands and arrange on top of the salad along with the prosciutto and the grilled peaches.

4 Top with a light drizzle of the balsamic glaze. Serve.

1 bunch lacinato kale, stemmed and roughly chopped
White Balsamic Vinaigrette (recipe follows)
Vegetable oil
3 large ripe peaches, pitted and quartered
1 ball burrata cheese
4 slices prosciutto
Balsamic Glaze (page 133)

White Balsamic Vinaigrette

YIELD: ABOUT 1 CUP

Place all the ingredients in a bowl and whisk well to combine.

¾ cup extra-virgin olive oil
¼ cup white balsamic vinegar
1 teaspoon Dijon mustard
1 teaspoon salt

Burrata is a fresh Italian cheese that has a hard mozzarella shell filled with soft mozzarella and cream. It's my absolute favorite of all the fresh cheeses.

Crustless Spring Quiche
with Asparagus, Mushrooms, and Goat Cheese

YIELD: 10 SERVINGS

My biggest brunch blunder ever came when I decided I would make a very large group of friends French omelets to order. I ended up so fixated on whisking and chopping that I hardly got to enjoy my own party. This is a solution that delivers all the egg-filled goodness with very little effort.

1 Adjust an oven rack to the middle position and preheat the oven to 400°F.

2 Grease a 9 x 13-inch baking dish with butter or spray with cooking spray, making sure to coat the bottom and sides.

3 On a rimmed baking sheet, drizzle the asparagus with olive oil and rub them to coat. Arrange them in an even layer and season them lightly with salt and pepper. Roast for 10 to 12 minutes, or until slightly charred.

4 Meanwhile, heat 2 tablespoons of olive oil in a large skillet over medium-high heat until shimmering. Add the mushrooms and season lightly with salt and pepper. Cook, tossing or stirring the mushrooms occasionally, for 5 to 7 minutes, or until nicely browned and all liquid has evaporated. Remove the skillet from the heat.

5 Transfer the asparagus pan to a cooling rack and allow to cool slightly.

1 tablespoon unsalted butter, at room temperature, or cooking spray

1 pound fresh asparagus, washed, woody ends trimmed, cut into 1-inch pieces

Olive oil

Salt and freshly ground black pepper

1 pound fresh mixed mushrooms, washed and sliced

6 ounces goat cheese (log type, such as chèvre) chilled and very thinly sliced

12 eggs, beaten

2 cups heavy cream

6   Arrange the asparagus in the prepared baking dish in a single layer, then top with a layer of mushrooms.

7   Remove the goat cheese from the fridge and break into bite-size chunks. Scatter the cheese evenly over the mushrooms.

8   Season the eggs with salt and pepper and beat them. Whisk in the cream and pour into the casserole. Bake for 35 to 40 minutes, or until the top is golden, the edges are puffy, and the center is just set. Transfer the casserole to a cooling rack and allow to cool at least 10 minutes before serving. Cut into squares and enjoy.

Keep the goat cheese chilled until ready to slice.
This can be made a few hours ahead and reheated when guests arrive.

Bananas Foster
French Toast

YIELD: 4 SERVINGS

Whenever I'm an invited guest for a weekend away, I sneak down
to the kitchen early on a Sunday morning and start assembling this dish. This
is a guaranteed crowd-pleaser. When your weary-eyed hosts show up
to the kitchen looking for coffee and are greeted by the sight of you whipping
these guys up, you know you'll always be welcomed back.

For the French toast:

1 Adjust an oven rack to the middle position and preheat the oven to 200°F.

2 Beat the eggs in a large bowl or casserole dish. Add the almond milk, vanilla, and salt and whisk until well combined.

3 Melt 2 tablespoons of the butter in a large skillet over medium heat until bubbling. Dip each croissant half into the egg mixture until well soaked. Cook two pieces, cut side down, for about 3 minutes per side or until evenly browned. Transfer to a rimmed baking sheet and keep warm in the oven. Repeat process with the remaining butter and pieces of croissant.

For the sauce:

1 In a medium-size skillet, heat the butter, sugar, and cinnamon over medium-low heat, stirring until the sugar has dissolved.

2 Stir in the banana liqueur, then add the banana slices and walnuts. Cook until the bananas are just warmed through and caramelized slightly, about 3 minutes.

3 Add the rum and cook until the rum is hot, then tip the pan away from you and carefully light with a match to flambé. Once the flame has died out, add the orange zest, spoon over the croissants, and enjoy right away.

FRENCH TOAST:
- **4 large eggs**
- **1 cup almond milk, whole milk, or heavy cream**
- **1 teaspoon pure vanilla extract**
- **Pinch salt**
- **4 tablespoons unsalted butter, cut into 4 pieces**
- **2 day-old croissants, cut in half lengthwise**

SAUCE:
- **3 tablespoons unsalted butter**
- **½ cup packed dark brown sugar**
- **½ teaspoon ground cinnamon**
- **¼ cup banana liqueur**
- **4 ripe but firm bananas, peeled and cut in half crosswise, then lengthwise**
- **½ cup walnuts, coarsely chopped**
- **¼ cup dark rum**
- **Finely grated zest of ½ orange**

I love using day-old croissants because you can get a deal on them at the market and they also do a better job of absorbing all the beautiful flavors of the egg mixture.

Be cautious to tip the pan away from you when you go to flambé. Don't be tempted to blow out the flame; it will naturally die out very quickly.

Japanese
Fried Chicken

Chicken and waffles is a classic tradition that goes way, way back.
I love twisting those traditions and shifting people's perceptions of what a
dish can become. This is my Far East take on a very southern staple.

For the chicken:

1 With a sharp paring knife, cut alongside the bones of the chicken thighs until you can remove them. Cut the thighs into 2-inch chunks.

2 In a large bowl, whisk together the ginger, garlic, tamari, mirin, scallion, and pepper. Add the chicken and toss to coat. Cover tightly with plastic wrap and marinate in the fridge for at least 2 hours. Remove the chicken from the fridge 30 minutes prior to cooking.

3 In a Dutch oven or other large, heavy-bottomed pot, heat the oil over medium-high heat to 360°F.

Set a wire rack over a baking sheet and cover with three layers of paper towels.

4 Place the potato starch in a large bowl or pie plate. Remove the chicken pieces from the marinade, gently shaking off the excess. Dredge them in the potato starch, shaking off the excess.

5 Working in batches to avoid overcrowding the pot, fry the chicken for about 7 minutes, or until deep golden brown. With a spider or metal slotted spoon, transfer the chicken to the prepared rack to drain.

To serve: Serve with the Matcha Green Tea Waffles, Ginger Maple Butter, Tonkatsu sauce, and Pickled Red Chile.

CHICKEN

4 bone-in, skin-on chicken thighs

1 (2-inch) piece fresh ginger, finely grated (about 1 tablespoon)

1 garlic clove, finely grated

3 tablespoon tamari or coconut aminos

1 tablespoon mirin

1 scallion, thinly sliced

½ teaspoon freshly ground black pepper

2 quarts canola oil

1 cup potato starch

TO SERVE:

Matcha Green Tea Waffles (page 180)

Ginger Maple Butter (recipe follows)

Tonkatsu sauce

Pickled Red Chile (recipe follows)

Pickled Red Chile

YIELD: ¾ CUP

1 long red chile, thinly sliced
½ cup red wine vinegar

Combine the chile and vinegar in a jar to marinate. Keeps indefinitely.

Ginger Maple Butter

YIELD: ABOUT 1½ CUPS BUTTER

1 cup pure maple syrup
8 ounces unsalted butter, chilled and cut into small cubes
1 (2-inch) piece fresh ginger, finely grated (about 1 tablespoon)
Salt

1 In a small saucepan over medium heat, gently warm the maple syrup just below a simmer.

2 Slowly whisk the butter, a few pieces at a time, into the maple syrup until it is emulsified. Whisk in the ginger and salt to taste. Set aside and cover to keep warm.

3 Store leftovers in an airtight container for up to 1 week in the fridge. Reheat in a small saucepan prior to serving.

Serve with the Matcha Green Tea Waffles (page 180) for the ultimate alternative to boring chicken and waffles.

Tonkatsu sauce is a Japanese barbecue sauce that usually accompanies fried pork cutlets. I love the sweet tang it brings to fried foods. It can be found in most Asian markets.

Matcha *Green Tea Waffles*

YIELD: 4 TO 6 WAFFLES (DEPENDING ON YOUR IRON)

These beautiful little green-hued waffles are loaded with antioxidants
and pack quite the caffeine kick. They are a natural
pairing with the Japanese Fried Chicken (page 176).

1 Preheat your waffle iron to medium-high.

2 In a large bowl, whisk together the flour, sugar, tea powder, baking powder, and salt.

3 In a separate bowl, whisk together the egg yolks and yogurt; set aside.

4 Using a whisk or electric mixer, whip the egg whites to firm peaks.

5 Stir the yogurt mixture into the flour mixture. Stir in the butter.

With a rubber spatula, gently stir in one-third of the egg whites. Fold in the remaining egg whites just until incorporated, being careful not to over mix.

6 Spray your waffle iron with cooking spray and spoon about ½ cup of batter onto it.

7 Cook until golden brown and slightly crisp, about 3 minutes.

8 Serve immediately or place in a preheated 200°F oven if making in batches.

2 cups gluten-free flour
3 tablespoons granulated sugar
1½ to 2 tablespoons matcha green tea powder
1 tablespoon baking powder
1 teaspoon salt
2 large eggs, separated
1 cup plain yogurt (not Greek)
6 tablespoons unsalted butter, melted and slightly cooled
Cooking spray
Ginger Maple Butter (page 177)

Make a big batch of these and freeze them individually.
When you're pressed for time, just pop them into the toaster
or oven to reheat.

Winter Squash and *Eggplant Gratin*

YIELD: 6 TO 8 SERVINGS

Most brunch items always seem so spring or summery; this is a great option for your next winter brunch. Squashes contain large amounts of vitamins A and C, which are crucial to keeping you healthy in the colder months.

FRIED PEPITAS:

1 cup olive oil
1 cup pepitas (pumpkin seeds)
Salt

GRATIN:

2 tablespoons duck fat or olive oil
2 garlic cloves, unpeeled and smashed
2 thyme sprigs
1 rosemary sprig
2 pounds winter squash, such as kobocha, pumpkin, or butternut, seeds and membranes removed, cut into ½-inch dice
1 medium-size eggplant, cut into 1-inch dice
Salt and freshly ground black pepper
Pecorino-Romano cheese, sliced with a vegetable peeler

For the pepitas: Line a plate with three layers of paper towels. Heat the oil in a medium-size saucepan over medium-high heat until shimmering. Add the pepitas and salt and fry, stirring constantly, until they start to puff up and turn golden, 3 to 4 minutes. Once they start popping, remove the saucepan from the heat. Using a slotted spoon, scoop the pepitas into a bowl to cool slightly.

For the gratin:

1 Adjust an oven rack to the bottom third of the oven and preheat the oven to 400°F.

2 Melt the duck fat in a Dutch oven or other heavy-bottomed pot until shimmering.

3 Add the garlic, thyme, and rosemary and cook until fragrant, about 1 minute, Add the squash and eggplant and stir to coat in the fat. Season with a good pinch of salt and a few grinds of pepper. Cover the pot and roast the vegetables for about 45 minutes, or until tender, stirring every 10 minutes.

4 Remove from the oven and gently mash the vegetables with a spoon or the back of a fork. Scoop into individual ramekins or a 9 x 13-inch baking dish and top with long strips of cheese. Top with the fried pepitas and place back in the oven for 2 minutes, or until the cheese melts.

The fried pepitas and their oil make a killer pesto (page 118).

Poached Salmon
with Mustard-Mint Sauce and Fingerling Potatoes

YIELD: 6 SERVINGS

Food is the best gift in life. One year I decided to fly home and surprise my mom for Mother's Day. I created a special menu just for her with all the ingredients she loves. I sent her out of the house to return to a beautifully set table with this gorgeous fish presentation at the center. We all opened a bottle of wine, laughed, and told embarrassing stories about times gone by. The day and the meal were perfection.

For the salmon: Place the carrots, celery, onion, dill, parsley, tarragon, and lemon slices in a large, shallow pot, wide enough to fit the salmon in an even layer later. Cover the vegetables with the water and wine. Bring the mixture to a boil over medium-high heat, lower the heat to medium-low, and simmer for 20 minutes. Prepare the potatoes and the sauce while the vegetables cook.

For the potatoes: Meanwhile, place the potatoes in a medium-size saucepan and cover with cold water. Add the garlic, thyme, rosemary, and 2 teaspoons of salt. Bring to a boil over medium-high heat, lower the heat to medium, and simmer for about 10 minutes, or until the potatoes are easily pierced by a knife. Drain the potatoes and when they're cool enough to handle, peel them (the skin should be easily removed with your fingertips) and cut them in half lengthwise.

SALMON:

- **2 carrots, peeled and cut into ½-inch chunks**
- **2 celery stalks, cut into ½-inch chunks**
- **1 small yellow onion, sliced**
- **3 dill sprigs, plus more for garnish**
- **2 parsley sprigs**
- **2 tarragon sprigs**
- **1 lemon, sliced**
- **2 cups water**
- **2 cups dry white wine**
- **2 pounds skin-on wild salmon, pin bones removed**

FINGERLING POTATOES:

¾ pound fingerling potatoes, scrubbed

3 garlic cloves, unpeeled and smashed

2 thyme sprigs

1 rosemary sprig

Salt

MUSTARD-MINT SAUCE:

1 cup fresh mint leaves

3 tablespoons sherry vinegar

2 large egg yolks

1 tablespoon whole-grain mustard

Salt

¾ cup extra-virgin olive oil

TO SERVE:

4 romaine hearts, cut into 4-inch lengths

6 cherry tomatoes, quartered

For the sauce:

1 Place the mint, vinegar, egg yolks, mustard, and a pinch of salt in a food processor and process until smooth. With the machine running, slowly drizzle in the oil through the feed tube until you have a thick and creamy sauce. Transfer the sauce to a bowl, season it with salt, and set aside.

2 Once the vegetable mixture has simmered for 20 minutes, slip the salmon into the pan, skin side up, and spoon the vegetables and liquid over it. Cover the pan with a lid and lower the heat to medium-low. Gently simmer for 6 to 8 minutes, depending on how cooked you like your salmon.

3 Using a spatula, carefully remove the salmon and place it, skin side up, on a cutting board. Remove the skin and flip the salmon back over, gently breaking it into pieces. Discard the vegetables.

4 Lay the romaine hearts on a serving platter. Scatter the potatoes around, then place the salmon pieces on top. Drizzle with the sauce and garnish with the quartered tomatoes and additional dill fronds. Serve.

Red Sangria

Chapter 8

Bar Cart:
Cocktails and Mixers

When I worked for Jean-Georges, I learned the importance of high-quality homemade syrups and mixers. I was exposed to exotic flavors that broadened both my mind and my palette. These staples work well in a cocktail, soda, or even as a base for sorbet.

Sometimes you want to drown your sorrows, sometimes you want to fix a cocktail for a new friend. Syrups, sodas, mixers...every celebration and everyone deserve a signature cocktail. This chapter shows you how to create your own signature cocktail or mocktail that you can be proud of.

Skinny *Strawberry Basil Margarita*

YIELD: 1 SERVING

1 tablespoon quartered fresh
strawberries

1 fresh basil leaf, plus 1 sprig,
for garnish

Ice

3 ounces tequila

2 ounces freshly squeezed lime
juice

2 ounces Strawberry Basil
Simple Syrup (recipe follows)

1 Place the strawberries and the basil leaf in the bottom of a rocks glass. Gently muddle with a muddler or just use a spoon, making sure you bash the basil well to release the fragrant oils.

2 Top with ice and add the tequila, lime juice, and syrup.

3 Stir well to combine, garnish with a sprig of basil.

Strawberry Basil Simple Syrup

YIELD: ABOUT 3 CUPS

1 cup fresh basil leaves

2 cups strawberries, hulled and
quartered

1 cup agave nectar

1 cup water

> Don't you dare throw away those used strawberries! They are amazing to muddle into the Skinny Strawberry Margarita (recipe above), drizzle over angel food cake for an easy dessert, or for tossing over your boring oatmeal. Now you've got a party!

1 Place the basil in the bottom of a large glass container (I used my 4-cup measuring cup).

2 In a medium-size saucepan, combine the strawberries, agave, and water.

3 Bring the mixture to a boil, lower the heat to a gentle simmer, and simmer for about 30 minutes.

4 Pour the hot syrup over the basil leaves and cover tightly with plastic wrap.

5 Allow the syrup to cool at room temperature and then place it in the fridge to marinate overnight.

6 Strain through a fine-mesh sieve or cocktail strainer.

7 Will keep covered in the fridge for a week.

Drunk in Love

YIELD: 1 SERVING

There is a lyric in a Beyoncé song where she sings about
"drinking watermelon" and I always wondered what that was about.
Instead of trying to track a very busy woman down, I decided
to create a summer cocktail in her honor.

1 In the bottom of a rocks glass, muddle the watermelon cubes and syrup.

2 Add ice, pour in the tequila over, and top with champagne.

3 Garnish with a basil leaf.

2 (1-inch) cubes seedless watermelon

2 ounces Basil Lime Simple Syrup (recipe follows)

Ice

2 ounces Herradura Silver Tequila

Champagne

1 fresh basil leaf, for garnish

Basil Lime Simple Syrup

YIELD: ABOUT 1½ CUPS SYRUP

1 In a medium-size saucepan, bring the lime juice and sugar to a boil, whisking to dissolve the sugar completely.

2 Place the basil leaves in a large glass jar or heatproof bowl and pour the syrup over them.

3 Cover tightly with plastic wrap and allow to steep for at least 4 hours.

1 cup freshly squeezed lime juice

1 cup granulated sugar

1 cup tightly packed fresh basil leaves

Kaffir Lime Simple Syrup

YIELD: A LITTLE MORE THAN 2 CUPS SYRUP

1½ cups kaffir lime leaves
1½ cups granulated sugar
1 cup freshly squeezed lime
  juice
½ cup water

1   Place the kaffir lime leaves and sugar in a food processor and process until the leaves are finely ground. Transfer the mixture to a medium-size saucepan, stir in the lime juice and water, and bring to a simmer over medium heat. Stir until the sugar has completely dissolved, then continue to simmer for 15 minutes.

2   Remove from the heat and allow the ingredients to meld at room temperature at least 2 hours. Strain the mixture through a fine-mesh strainer. Use immediately or store in an airtight container for up to 1 week in the fridge.

> This works great in a cocktail, but if you mix it with sparkling water or champagne and freeze, it makes a killer Popsicle.

Lemongrass Simple Syrup

YIELD: ABOUT 2 CUPS SYRUP

1 cup agave nectar
1 cup water
3 stalks lemongrass, tops and
  bottoms trimmed, exterior
  layers removed, tender middle
  thinly sliced.

1   Whisk the agave and water together in a small saucepan. Stir in the lemongrass and bring to a boil over medium-high heat, then lower the heat to medium and simmer for 15 minutes.

2   Remove the saucepan from the heat and cover tightly with a lid or foil and allow to come to room temperature, at least 4 hours.

3   Once cool, strain the syrup through a fine-mesh sieve into a glass bottle or jar. Use immediately or store in an airtight container for up to 2 weeks in the fridge.

> Swap this for the Lavender Simple Syrup, for a fresh twist on the Frozen Lavender Latte (page 79).

Cocoa Champagne

YIELD: 8 TO 10 COCKTAILS

This reminds me of the two things I loved most about traveling around Paris: the chocolate and the champagne. The combination may sound strange, but these two are a natural fit.

1 cup granulated sugar

1 cup high-quality unsweetened cocoa powder

1 cup water

Small pinch of salt

Fresh raspberries

Champagne or sparkling wine

1 In a small saucepan, whisk together the sugar and cocoa powder, whisk in the water, and bring to a simmer over medium-high heat. Simmer for about 5 minutes, whisking to dissolve the sugar completely. Remove from the heat and let cool completely. Store sealed in an airtight jar.

2 Place 2 raspberries in the bottom of each champagne glass and pour in 1 tablespoon of the syrup. Top with champagne.

> This syrup goes great in coffee or over ice cream.

Lemon-Thyme
Ginger Beer

YIELD: 12 COCKTAILS

This syrup works well in a number of cocktails, and topped with sparkling water, makes an amazingly refreshing soda! Have some fun and experiment; let me know what you think.

For the syrup:

1 Stir the lemon juice and sugar together in a small saucepan. Bring the mixture to a simmer over medium heat, stirring until the sugar is completely dissolved.

2 Place the thyme sprigs and ginger in a heatproof container, pour the lemon syrup over them, and cover with a tight-fitting lid. Chill for at least 8 hours in the fridge. Use immediately or store for up to 2 weeks.

To serve: Pour 2 ounces of syrup into a champagne flute and top with sparkling white wine or pour into a glass and top with sparkling water.

SYRUP:

- **1½ cups freshly squeezed lemon juice, strained**
- **1½ cups granulated sugar, or 1¼ cups agave nectar**
- **7 fresh thyme sprigs**
- **1½ cups peeled and chopped fresh ginger**

TO SERVE:

- **Sparkling white wine or sparkling water, chilled**

Be careful not to overcook the lemon juice and sugar mixture, as it will dull the acidic zing of the lemon.

Autumn *Mimosa*

This sparkling autumn cocktail is like biting into a boozy spiced apple.
It's the perfect drink to welcome your friends for a fall gathering.

SPICED SIMPLE SYRUP:
- **1 cup apple cider**
- **1 cup packed dark brown sugar**
- **8 fresh sage leaves**
- **½ bunch thyme sprigs, divided**
- **1 teaspoon pumpkin pie spice**

MIMOSAS:
- **1 cup freshly squeezed lemon juice, strained**
- **1 (750 ml) bottle champagne or other sparkling wine, chilled**

For the spiced simple syrup:

1 Combine the cider and sugar in a small saucepan and bring to a gentle simmer over medium-low heat. Cook, stirring, until the sugar is completely dissolved. Remove from the heat, stir in the sage, 3 thyme sprigs, and pumpkin pie spice. Cover and infuse at least 30 minutes.

2 Strain the syrup through a fine-mesh sieve and discard the solids. Chill in the fridge for at least 30 minutes. You can make the syrup up to 1 week in advance.

For the mimosas: Pour 1 ounce (2 tablespoons) each of the lemon juice and the simple syrup into a champagne flute and top with champagne.

Red *Sangria*

When throwing a party, don't get caught up making all your guests individual cocktails; batch-make this ahead of time, so you can enjoy the party as much as your guests will. If you want to keep your sangria chilled without being watered down, try freezing some grapes and tossing them into the sangria just as the guests are arriving. As they melt they will keep the wine chilled and add a flavorful element at the same time.

1 Place the oranges, apples, lime slices, and sugar in a large bowl and gently stir. Allow to macerate for 10 minutes.

2 Stir in the lime juice, wine, brandy, and Grand Marnier. Allow the mixture to rest in the fridge overnight, if time allows.

Otherwise, immediately top with sparkling water or seltzer and serve on ice.

3 You can make the base and pour it into small vessels, topping with the sparkling water or seltzer just before serving to keep the fizz.

- 3 oranges, cut into quarter-moons
- 2 apples, cored and thinly sliced into half-moons
- 2 limes: 1 thinly sliced, 1 juiced
- ¾ cup caster or superfine sugar
- 3 (750 ml) bottles inexpensive dry red wine (I like rioja or tempranillo), chilled
- 1½ cups brandy
- ½ cup Grand Marnier
- 1½ liters sparkling water or seltzer water, chilled
- Ice

Blackberry Shrub

YIELD: ABOUT 2½ CUPS SHRUB

This is a great combination of sweet and sour and I like to use it as a mixer for cocktails. It's a wonderful substitution for those who choose not to imbibe. I like using coconut palm sugar for its rich toasted notes and it also won't spike your insulin like regular sugar.

1 cup blackberries, plus a few more for garnish

1 cup coconut palm sugar

1 cup fresh basil leaves

1 cup champagne or white balsamic vinegar

TO SERVE:

Champagne or sparkling water, chilled

1 Combine the blackberries, sugar, basil, and vinegar in a large jar or container with a tight-fitting lid, shake vigorously, and let stand at room temperature for 2 days, shaking from time to time.

2 Strain through a mesh sieve into a clean container and store for up to 3 weeks in the fridge.

3 Place 2 ounces of the shrub in a champagne glass and top with 6 to 8 ounces of champagne or sparkling water.

Having a premade batch on hand will ensure that you are always ready for unexpected guests.

Herb-Stuffed Branzino
with Tahini Yogurt

Chapter 9

Getting Back Out There with a Bang: *Dinners, Celebrations, and Get-Togethers*

When planning a party, be creative but also try to be mindful of who may be showing up—this time it's not *all* about you.

Oh yeah: That time I almost killed Nicole Kidman....

It's not every day that Nicole Kidman and Keith Urban come over to your house for a spot of tea and some breakfast. When they did say they were popping by, I knew I couldn't just throw a couple of toaster strudels in the oven and call it a day. I went and pulled out all the stops.

Now, I'm a little obsessive and a perfectionist as it is, but whipping up a meal for one of the most beautiful and talented actresses of our day and her equally talented beau took me to a whole 'nother level of crazy!

At this point, my culinary skills were still very modest. I didn't have the dexterity and skill that has come with the thousands of hours of practice that I have accrued now. I took my little paring knife, and I must have spent a good 45 minutes whittling grapefruits until they were perfectly symmetrical, hollow bowls. I had created the perfect vessel for what was to be the greatest fruit salad ever dreamed of.

Everything was in there. I started with a beautiful grapefruit and mint simple syrup. There were no fruits left behind. There was pineapple, grapefruit, banana, pomegranate, orange, apple, grapes, and delicious, ripe strawberries. At this point, even Carmen Miranda's hat would have been jealous! To top it off, it was garnished with the freshest of fresh mint plucked straight from my backyard herb garden and more thinly sliced fresh strawberries. It was absolute perfection in fruit bowl form.

As I proudly carried these on a tray toward my distinguished guests, I suddenly noticed a look of fear and panic coming over Nicole's face. She looked uncomfortable, and she wriggled in her seat. Oh my god, what had I done? She hadn't even tasted it! She could barely even smell the delicious herbs from where I stood! She calmly reached for her purse and removed something. I was baffled at this odd reaction but kept smiling and trying to play it cool. I placed the fruit bowl in front of her.

"I'm allergic to strawberries," she said graciously in her beautiful Australian accent as she waved her EpiPen at me.

"FUCK ME," I remarked under my breath in my pseudo-midwestern cum Californian way—while still holding a smile. Thankfully, she was not allergic to the beautiful goat cheese and roasted asparagus omelet that followed. If I can share one bit of advice, it would be: Always ask your guests if they have any food allergies before you cleverly start whittling away for hours.

Shrimp Salsa

YIELD: 4 TO 6 SERVINGS

These are great at a party or just your everyday lunch.

4 vine-ripe tomatoes, finely diced

1 small red onion, finely diced (6 tablespoons)

1 to 2 jalapeño peppers, seeds and ribs removed, finely diced

2 tablespoons minced fresh cilantro

Juice of 2 limes

1 pound cooked, peeled shrimp, finely diced

½ teaspoon salt

1 head iceberg lettuce, leaves pulled apart and trimmed into 5-inch "cups"

1   In a large bowl, combine the tomatoes, onion, jalapeños (to taste), cilantro, and lime juice. Let the mixture sit for 5 minutes. Stir in the shrimp and season to taste with salt. Cover with plastic wrap and refrigerate for 1 hour to let the flavors combine.

2   Serve inside the lettuce cups.

How To: *Lobster*

1 Find a pot that can comfortably hold the amount of lobsters you wish to cook. Add water to cover. I usually aim for 3 quarts of water per lobster. Season the water aggressively with sea salt until it tastes like the ocean (½ to ¾ cup works for 3 quarts; scale accordingly).

2 Bring the water to a strong boil, lower the heat to a gentle boil, then slip in the live lobsters, cooking, uncovered, for about 8 minutes. Remove from the heat and allow to rest for another 5 minutes before cracking.

Lobster Lettuce Cups

YIELD: 4 SERVINGS

This is like holding summer in your hand. I've served these at my summer parties almost every year since I moved to New York City.

1 lobster, cooked (see How To, previous page)

1 celery stalk, peeled and very finely diced

1 cornichon or ¼ pickle, finely diced (about 1 teaspoon)

Salt and freshly ground black pepper

3 tablespoons ketchup

3 tablespoons Spicy Mayo (page 34)

Finely grated zest of ½ lemon plus 1 tablespoon juice

2 teaspoons fresh tarragon, minced

1 head iceberg lettuce, leaves pulled apart and trimmed into 5-inch "cups"

1   Cut the lobster meat into bite-size pieces and place them in a large bowl. Gently stir in the celery and cornichon, season with salt and pepper, and set aside.

2   In a medium-size bowl, whisk together the ketchup, Spicy Mayo, and lemon zest and juice.

3   Pour the mixture over the lobster and gently stir with a rubber spatula until all the lobster is evenly coated. Sprinkle with the tarragon and stir just to combine.

4   Spoon into the lettuce cups and serve at once.

Sticky Oven-Baked
Chicken Wings

YIELD: 4 SERVINGS

I always make sure to have a big batch of these made when I have friends over to watch a big game. Invited to a potluck and don't know what to bring? Problem solved. These will make you friends faster than you could ever imagine.

WINGS:

- **2 pounds chicken wings**
- **½ cup tamari**
- **1 (1-inch) piece fresh ginger, finely grated (2 tablespoons)**
- **2 tablespoons chili garlic paste**
- **2 tablespoons mirin**
- **2 teaspoons sesame oil**
- **1 teaspoon Asian fish sauce**
- **Grapeseed or other high-heat oil**

CHILI GLAZE:

- **1 recipe Sriracha Chile Glaze (page 153)**
- **Finely grated zest and juice of ½ lime**

TO SERVE:

- **6 scallions, sliced**
- **Toasted sesame seeds**

For the wings:

1. Trim the wing tips off the wings and discard them or reserve them to make chicken stock. Cut the wings at the first joint to separate them into the classic "wings" and "drumettes."

2. In a large bowl or gallon-size resealable plastic bag, combine the tamari, ginger, chili garlic paste, mirin, sesame oil, and fish sauce. Add the wings, toss together in the bowl or shake in the bag to thoroughly coat, and store in the fridge at least 4 hours, and up to overnight for more intense flavor.

3. When ready to cook, adjust two oven racks to the top and middle positions and preheat the oven to 450°F. Set a wire rack inside a rimmed baking sheet. Place the wings on the prepared sheet and discard the marinade. Drizzle with oil and roast on the middle rack for 25 minutes, or until cooked through.

For the glaze:

1. While the wings are in the oven, whisk the Sriracha Chile Glaze and lime zest together in a large bowl. Add the wings to the bowl and toss to evenly coat them.

2. Set the oven to broil. Return the wings to the sheet pan broil them for 2 to 3 minutes (timing will depend on your broiler, so keep an eye on them), or until caramelized.

To serve: Drizzle with any remaining glaze and top with the sliced scallions and toasted sesame seeds.

Paleo *Nachos*

From the moment I made the duck fat chips, I knew I wanted to make them into nachos. Layered high in spicy taco meat, tomatoes, and guacamole, these are the perfect complement to your next tailgate or Netflix binge.

For the taco seasoning: In a medium-size bowl, stir together the chili powder, cumin, arrowroot, salt, paprika, Aleppo, coriander, and onion powder. This seasoning can be stored in an airtight container for up to 3 months at room temperature.

For the beef:

1 Heat 1 tablespoon oil in a large skillet over medium-high heat until shimmering. Add half of the scallions and half of the diced tomatoes, and cook, stirring, for 3 minutes.

2 Add the meat and cook, stirring and breaking up the meat, for 8 minutes, or until lightly browned. Stir in 1½ tablespoons of the taco seasoning and the serrano, if using, and continue to cook for another 3 minutes, making sure to combine well. Remove from the heat and set aside.

To assemble: Arrange a layer of chips on a large platter. Top with the meat, yogurt, if using, and guacamole. Finish with the tomatillo salsa, pickled jalapeños, and remaining scallions and tomatoes.

TACO SEASONING:
- **2 tablespoons chili powder**
- **1 tablespoon ground cumin**
- **2 teaspoons arrowroot powder**
- **2 teaspoons salt**
- **1 teaspoon smoked paprika**
- **½ teaspoon Aleppo pepper or red pepper flakes**
- **½ teaspoon ground coriander**
- **½ teaspoon onion powder**

BEEF:
- **Olive oil**
- **2 scallions, thinly sliced**
- **2 plum tomatoes, diced**
- **1 pound lean ground beef, pork, or turkey**
- **½ serrano chile, seeds and ribs removed, chopped (optional)**

FOR ASSEMBLY:
- **Duck Fat Sweet Potato Chips (page 124)**
- **Greek yogurt (optional; skip for strict Paleo diets)**
- **Guacamole (page 40)**
- **Roasted Tomatillo Salsa (page 27)**
- **Pickled jalapeños**

Spicy *Duck Tacos*

YIELD: 4 SERVINGS

This is a great way to use any leftover duck from the Duck Fried Rice (page 64).

½ cup nonfat Greek yogurt

2 teaspoons harissa paste

Finely grated zest and juice of
   1 lime

Salt

1 Muscovy duck breast, cooked
   and thinly sliced (see How To,
   page 62)

4 Paleo Crêpes (page 35)

½ red onion, thinly sliced

1 radish, julienned

½ cup fresh cilantro leaves

1. In a medium bowl, whisk together the yogurt, harissa, lime zest and juice, and a pinch of salt; set aside.

2. Divide the thinly sliced duck among the Paleo crêpes and top with the spicy yogurt sauce, red onion, radish, and cilantro. Serve.

Herb-Stuffed Branzino
with Tahini Yogurt

YIELD: 1 TO 2 SERVINGS

This reminds me of my first trip to MachneYuda Market in Jerusalem. I was literally running from stall to stall to see who had the best of what. I was overwhelmed by the selection of fish, produce, and dairy and I had a great time haggling with the purveyors in my broken Hebrew. This is the meal I cooked for my friends and family on a beautiful balmy Middle Eastern night. I originally cooked this outside over a hot charcoal grill, or *al ha'esh*, as they say in Hebrew. The cook time is about the same. Living in a New York apartment, I don't have access to a grill all the time, so I adapted this recipe for the oven so I could enjoy this roasted fish any time of year.

1 branzino, scaled and cleaned
Olive oil
Salt and freshly ground black pepper
1 small rosemary sprig
1 fresh thyme sprig
1 bay leaf
1 lemon, halved: ½ thinly sliced, ½ left intact
Minted Couscous (page 225)
2 tablespoons Marcona almonds, chopped
Fresh chopped parsley, for garnish
Tahini Yogurt (page 31)
Pomegranate molasses (optional)

1. Preheat the oven to 500°F. Adjust the oven rack to the middle position.

2. Rub the fish with olive oil, season the flesh and the cavity of the fish well with salt and pepper. Place on a sheet pan.

3. Stuff the fish with the herbs and sliced lemon.

4. Rub the cut side of the remaining lemon half with olive oil and place, cut side down, on the sheet pan next to the branzino.

5. Roast for 12 minutes, flipping halfway through, until the skin is crisp and the flesh pulls away easily.

6. Serve on top of the Minted Couscous with almonds, fresh parsley, roasted lemon, Tahini Yogurt, and a drizzle of pomegranate molasses.

Oven-Smoked *Ribs*

YIELD: 6 TO 8 SERVINGS

No grill? No problem! This is perfect when it's the height of barbecue season. Don't worry if you don't have access to a grill or smoker; with these easy techniques you can get the same flavor as ribs that have been smoked twice as long! Cooking the ribs inside will give you more room on the grill for burgers and dogs. Everybody wins!
First things first: Make your rub. I like to use a brown sugar–based rub that has a smoky kick to it. Most of these ingredients are probably already in your pantry; if not, they can all be found in any supermarket.

PORK RIB DRY RUB:
- **1 cup packed dark brown sugar**
- **¼ cup dry mustard**
- **2 teaspoons granulated garlic**
- **2 teaspoons onion powder**
- **2 teaspoons smoked paprika**
- **1½ teaspoons cayenne pepper (you can use less if you want less heat)**
- **2 teaspoons salt**

RIBS:
- **2 (3-pound) racks baby back ribs, trimmed of the sinuous flap on the back (if you don't how to do this is ask, your butcher to remove it)**
- **1 bag hickory wood smoking chips**
- **Your favorite barbecue sauce— I prefer a combination of Stubbs and Sweet Baby Ray's**

For the rub: With a whisk or fork, combine the brown sugar, mustard, granulated garlic, onion powder, paprika, and cayenne in a medium-size bowl. Store in an airtight container until ready to use. The rub will keep for up to 1 month.

For the ribs:

1. Rub a generous amount of the pork rub over both sides of the ribs, making sure to pat it down with your hands to make a "crust." You can do this the night before, to flavor the ribs even more. Wrap the racks tightly in plastic wrap and store in the fridge.

2. When ready to cook, adjust an oven rack to the topmost position (it should be about 6 inches from the flame), and a second oven rack to the middle position. Turn the broiler to HIGH. Turn on the exhaust fan if you have one.

3. Line a rimmed baking sheet with foil and spread an even layer of the hickory chips on it. Place the pan under the broiler and let the chips develop a nice char on them, but be careful not to ignite them!

Continued . . .

4   Transfer the baking sheet to a cooling rack, add 1 cup of water to the pan, and place the wire rack on top. Place the ribs directly onto the wire rack and wrap the tray tightly in aluminum foil.

5   Adjust the oven temperature to 285°F. Cook the ribs for 2 hours 30 minutes. Transfer the baking sheet to a cooling rack and carefully peel back the foil to let the steam and smoke escape. Using tongs, transfer the ribs to a clean baking sheet.

6   Return to the broiler setting to HIGH. Slather the ribs with your favorite barbecue sauce and run the ribs under the broiler until the sauce becomes bubbly and starts to caramelize, 5 to 7 minutes; be sure to keep an eye on them, as broilers' intensity levels vary.

7   Before serving, slather a little more sauce on the ribs. Carve and enjoy!

Slow-Baked
Tenderloin

YIELD: 8 TO 10 SERVINGS

My mother once called me, freaking out about how to cook steak
for a large group. She had her heart set on filet, but she was intimidated
by the timing of cooking that many individual steaks.
Of course, I talked her from that ledge and gave her a few tips and words
of encouragement when it comes to cooking for large groups.
This is my simplified version of the usually labor-intensive endeavor
of cooking a million steaks at once. I said, "Mom, have a glass of wine
and let the oven do all the work!" Sit back and enjoy some wine and
conversation with friends; you've earned it.

1 (2- to 2½-pound) beef tenderloin, trimmed and tied by your butcher
Salt and freshly ground black pepper
3 tablespoons olive oil
3 tablespoons butter
3 garlic cloves
4 thyme sprigs
Maldon salt

1. Adjust an oven rack to the middle position and preheat the oven to 275°F. Set a wire rack inside a rimmed baking sheet.

2. Two hours before cooking, generously season the steak with salt and pepper. Place it, unwrapped, in the fridge to chill. This salting process will greatly enhance the delicious crust formed in the final process.

3. Pull the tenderloin out of the fridge 30 minutes before cooking.

4. Place the meat on the prepared baking sheet pan and cook for 2 to 2½ hours, or until an internal thermometer placed in the thickest part registers 125°F. Transfer the baking sheet to a cooling rack.

5. Heat the oil in a large skillet over medium-high heat until just beginning to smoke. Brown the meat on all sides, then lower the heat and toss in the butter, garlic, and thyme. Baste the meat all over as you cook for 2 minutes more. Transfer the meat to a serving tray and pour the pan juices over it. Allow to rest at least 5 minutes, then cut into 1-inch-thick slices. Finish with Maldon salt, and serve.

Lemon and Herb–Roasted *Sunchokes*

YIELD: 4 SERVINGS

You may not be familiar with these tasty little tubers, but I guarantee after making these once, you will be hooked. The inulin starch in these vitamin-loaded earthy treats makes a great potato alternative for people with diabetes. These are also approved for those on strict Paleo diets and are often referred to as "Paleo potatoes."

1 Adjust an oven rack to the middle position and preheat the oven to 400°F.

2 In a medium-size bowl, toss the sunchokes together with the rosemary and thyme and season with salt and pepper. Drizzle with olive oil and toss to coat.

3 Place the sunchokes in a single layer on a baking sheet and cook until crispy on the outside and tender on the inside, about 50 minutes.

4 Put the sunchokes back in the bowl, add the lemon zest and juice, and toss to combine.

5 Season to taste with salt and pepper. Serve.

2 cups sunchokes, thoroughly scrubbed and cut into bite-size pieces
2 teaspoons fresh rosemary, minced
1 teaspoon fresh thyme leaves
Salt and freshly ground black pepper
2 tablespoons olive oil
Juice and zest of ½ lemon

These are a perfect side to the Cocoa and Coffee–Encrusted Rib Eye Steak (page 70).

Fingerling *Potato Salad*

YIELD: 8 SERVINGS

The lightness of the fresh herb dressing is a welcome change from the mayo-based salads my mom used to make. This salad provides a perfect complement to the rich, heavy grilled meats that are so prevalent in barbecue season. You may never go back to that heavily sauced mess again. Sorry, Mom, I still love you.

POTATOES:
- **6 pounds fingerling potatoes, scrubbed**
- **Salt**

DRESSING:
- **2 tablespoons Dijon mustard**
- **½ cup freshly squeezed lemon juice**
- **⅔ cup fresh flat-leaf parsley, finely chopped**
- **⅔ cup fresh basil leaves, finely chopped**
- **⅔ cup fresh cilantro, finely chopped**
- **2 large shallots, minced (about ¼ cup)**
- **Salt and freshly ground black pepper**
- **1½ cups extra-virgin olive oil**

TO SERVE:
- **1 small bunch chives, minced (about ¼ cup)**

For the potatoes:

1 Place the potatoes in a large pot. Add enough cold water to cover them by at least 2 inches (if you don't have a big enough pot, use two smaller ones). Add 3 tablespoons of salt.

2 Bring the potatoes and water to a boil over high heat, then lower the heat to medium, keeping the water at a simmer. Cook until they are easily pierced with the tip of a knife, but not mushy, about 15 minutes. Remove the pot from the heat, drain the potatoes in a colander set in the sink, and set them aside to cool slightly.

For the dressing: Meanwhile, in a medium-size bowl, whisk together the mustard and lemon juice. Stir in the parsley, basil, cilantro, and shallots, and season lightly with salt and pepper. Slowly whisk in the oil.

To serve:

1 Quarter the potatoes, place them in a large bowl, and season them with salt and pepper. Drizzle and toss them with enough dressing to thoroughly coat them. Allow the potato salad to sit for about 15 minutes prior to serving, to allow the dressing to properly flavor them.

2 Sprinkle them with the chives just before serving.

Don't give in to the mayo-laden salads of your past. This can be enjoyed any time of year and definitely won't weigh you down when it's hot out. Try this recipe with some lump crabmeat mixed in and serve topped with a beautiful piece of crisp, skinned salmon. It's also fun to roast the potatoes first and then toss them into the vinaigrette.

Rib Eye Beef Skewers,
No-Peanut Sauce, and Grilled Shishito Peppers

YIELD: 4 SERVINGS

2½ pounds well-marbled rib eye, cut into ½-inch cubes
Salt and freshly ground black pepper
Olive oil
1 pound shishito peppers
4 limes, cut in half
Maldon or other flaky sea salt
1 cup No-Peanut Sauce (page 72)

1. Heat a grill or grill pan to medium-high. Have ready metal skewers or bamboo skewers that have been soaked in water for 15 minutes.

2. Thread the meat on the skewers and season well with salt and pepper. Oil the grill and cook to medium rare, about 4 minutes per side, being careful not to burn the skewers (see note). Transfer them to a large serving platter and allow to rest 5 minutes.

3. While the beef is resting, toss the shishitos in just enough oil to coat them and lay them directly onto the hottest part of the grill. Cook until nicely charred, about 3 minutes per side. Transfer the shishitos to the platter. Place the limes, cut side down, on the grill and cook for 3 minutes, until charred. Season the peppers with Maldon salt. Drizzle the meat with No-Peanut Sauce and squeeze the charred limes over everything. Serve.

Wrap a side of the grill grate in aluminum foil and place the ends of your skewers over that side. This will prevent them from burning over an open flame.

Juniper-Encrusted Bison with Roasted Broccolini and Pickled Red Chile

This is an easy anytime meal that requires very little preplanning and comes together in about 20 minutes. I love pickled chile on almost everything, but they really do a great job brightening up the roasted flavors of the meat and vegetable.

JUNIPER SALT:

- **2 tablespoons juniper berries**
- **1 tablespoon Maldon salt**

BISON:

- **2 (6-ounce, 2-inch-thick) pieces bison tenderloin**
- **Freshly ground black pepper**
- **1 bunch broccolini**
- **Olive oil**
- **Pickled Red Chile (page 177)**

> If you can't find bison, use the leanest cut of beef you can find. Bringing the meat out 20 minutes before cooking will result in a more evenly cooked finished product.

For the juniper salt: Place the juniper berries and salt in a completely dry blender or spice grinder, cover tightly, and blend on high speed for 15 seconds, until finely ground.

For the bison:

1. Adjust an oven rack to the middle position and preheat the oven to 400°F.

2. Take the bison out of the fridge 20 minutes prior to cooking. Season it liberally with juniper salt and pepper; set aside.

3. Toss the broccolini in just enough oil to coat. Season it with salt and pepper and arrange in a single layer on a baking sheet. Roast for 20 to 25 minutes, or until just starting to get a deep char. Transfer the pan to a cooling rack.

4. Heat 1 tablespoon of oil in a large skillet over medium-high heat until just beginning to smoke. Place the bison pieces in the skillet, pressing down on them to make good contact with the pan. Cook for 4 minutes per side for rare. Transfer the bison to a cutting board and allow to rest for 4 minutes before slicing.

5. Serve on top of the broccolini and top with the Pickled Red Chile.

Oven-Roasted
Caprese

On a recent trip to Los Angeles, I was reminded and amazed that even in the dead of winter I could still pull together some tomatoes to make an amazing salad. If you happen to live in a cold climate like myself, don't stress—even average tomatoes become incredible after they are roasted in the oven!

For the roasted tomatoes:

1 Adjust an oven rack to the middle position and preheat the oven to 285°F.

2 In a large bowl, toss the quartered tomatoes in enough olive oil to coat. Season them with salt and pepper.

3 Arrange the tomatoes, skin side down, on a baking sheet and cook them until roasted, 35 to 40 minutes depending on your oven. They'll be a bit juicy. Transfer the baking sheet to a cooling rack and allow to cool to room temperature.

To assemble: Arrange the tomatoes on a plate with the cheese. Garnish with the basil and mint. Season with Maldon salt and pepper, drizzle with olive oil and Balsamic Glaze, and serve.

ROASTED TOMATOES:
- **6 Roma tomatoes, cored and quartered**
- **Extra-virgin olive oil**
- **Salt and freshly ground black pepper**

FOR ASSEMBLY:
- **6 ounces fresh mozzarella or burrata cheese, torn into pieces**
- **Fresh basil leaves**
- **Fresh mint leaves**
- **Maldon or other flaky sea salt**
- **Balsamic Glaze (page 133)**

> Enjoy this as is or oil up some good whole-wheat bread and toast it in a pan until golden and crispy, rub with a clove of garlic, and top with this aromatic salad.

Oven-Baked
Corn Chips

YIELD: 4 TO 6 SERVINGS

These chips are best eaten warm straight out of the oven with Roasted Tomatillo Salsa (page 27) or superfresh Guacamole (page 40). There are infinite options when it comes to seasoning these crisp chips, so feel free to play around with different salts and spices.

10 corn tortillas, cut into quarters
Cooking spray
Salt

1 Adjust an oven rack to the middle position and preheat the oven to 350°F.

2 Place the tortilla quarters on a baking sheet in a single layer and lightly spray them with cooking spray, making sure to coat each side evenly.

3 Bake for 15 minutes, or until they are crisp and golden. Transfer the baking sheet to a cooling rack and season the chips with salt. Enjoy.

These are the best right out of the oven, seasoned well with salt and a squeeze of lime.

Fish Taco Bar

YIELD: 4 SERVINGS

Fish tacos are party tacos, so call up your friends, fire up the grill, and chill out with a cold beverage. When choosing fish, select a nice flaky white fish that will absorb all of the delicious marinade.

For the fish:

1 In a medium-size bowl, whisk together the chili powder, oil, lime zest and juice, serrano, and cilantro. Place the fish in a container and pour the marinade over it. Cover the fish and allow it to marinate at room temperature for 20 minutes.

2 Heat a well-oiled grill pan over high heat, or adjust an oven rack to the top position and set the oven to broil. If using the broiler, make sure to coat the bottom of the tray with oil to avoid sticking.

3 Use a slotted spatula to remove the fish from the marinade, allowing the excess to drip off. Place the fish on the grill pan or prepared baking sheet and cook for about 2 minutes per side, or until the fish is opaque. Transfer to a plate and gently flake the fish apart with a fork.

To assemble: Serve the fish with the Avocado Crema, grilled corn tortillas, and any and all of the suggested condiments.

The fish is done when it looks translucent and just starts to flake apart. When buying avocados, look for the ones that are a deep greenish brown that give slightly when gently squeezed in the palm of your hand.

FISH:

1 tablespoon dark chili powder, such as ancho

¼ cup grapeseed or vegetable oil, plus more for the pan

Finely grated zest and juice of 2 limes

½ serrano chile, seeds and ribs removed, finely chopped

½ cup fresh cilantro leaves, chopped

1 pound flaky white fish (I like cod or mahimahi)

FOR ASSEMBLY:

Avocado Crema (page 31)

Cilantro leaves

Corn tortillas, grilled

Hot sauce (optional)

Lime wedges (optional)

Shallots, thinly sliced and soaked in red wine vinegar for 1 hour (optional)

Sliced red cabbage (optional)

Sliced scallions (optional)

Moroccan-Spiced Lamb
with Tahini Yogurt and Minted Couscous

YIELD: 2 TO 4 SERVINGS

MOROCCAN SPICE MIX:
- **2 tablespoons ground cumin**
- **1 tablespoon ground coriander**
- **1 tablespoon smoked paprika**
- **1 teaspoon ground allspice**
- **1 teaspoon ground cinnamon**
- **¼ teaspoon ground cloves**
- **Salt and freshly ground black pepper**
- **6 garlic cloves, grated (2 tablespoons)**

MINTED COUSCOUS:
- **1 cup homemade or low-sodium chicken stock**
- **1 cup plain couscous**
- **3 dates, pitted and finely diced**
- **10 fresh mint leaves**

LAMB:
- **1 rack of lamb, trimmed and frenched by your butcher**
- **3 tablespoons olive oil**
- **Tahini Yogurt (page 31)**
- **¼ cup pomegranate seeds**
- **¼ cup fresh flat-leaf parsley leaves**

For the Moroccan spice mix: In a small bowl, stir all the ingredients. Set aside.

For the minted couscous: Bring the chicken stock to a boil in a medium-size saucepan over medium-high heat. Place the couscous in a large bowl and pour the stock over it. Cover the bowl with plastic wrap and allow to steam for 5 minutes. Remove the plastic and fluff the couscous with a fork. Stir in the dates and mint and set aside.

For the lamb:

1 Cut the lamb into two double chop sections. Rub 3 tablespoons of the Moroccan spice mix all over the chops and store them in an airtight container overnight in the fridge to marinate.

2 Remove the chops from the fridge when ready to cook. Adjust an oven rack to the middle position and preheat the oven to 400°F. Place a cooling rack inside a rimmed baking sheet.

3 Heat the oil in a large skillet over medium-high heat until just beginning to smoke. Add the lamb chops, fat side down. Sear on all sides to form a nice crust, about 2 minutes per side. Transfer the chops to the prepared rack, fat side up, and cook for another 10 minutes, or until medium rare. Remove from the oven and allow to rest for 5 minutes. Slice each double chop in half.

4 Serve on top of the minted couscous and drizzle with tahini yogurt. Finish with the pomegranate seeds and parsley.

Chocolate Chip Cookies

Chapter 10

Sweet Somethings:
Desserts and Treats

The importance of sweets was instilled in me by my grandmother at a very early age. She was famous for making everything from tiny prune jam cookies to the most grand of wedding cakes. I also learned how sharing a sweet treat with people would elicit a response unlike any other. Learning how to bake was really my first step on the performing stage. The gratification is instant. There is no greater feeling than making something beautiful and sweet and then sharing it with someone you love. I cherish that instant when the first bite is taken; it's one of those fleeting moments of pure joy in this world for myself and the person doing the eating. So, go ahead and reward yourself with a Chocolate–Chocolate Chip Cookie with Salted Caramel Drizzle. As you decide with whom to share your sweets, remember: There are two types of people in this world. People who love warm freshly fried doughnuts, and people you don't want to be friends with.

Chocolate Chip Cookies

YIELD: ABOUT 2 DOZEN COOKIES

When I bake, I like to measure by weight instead of volume,
for absolute accuracy. This process produces faster, cleaner, and the most
consistent results. I have included the US conversion for those
who may not have a scale.

1 Adjust two oven racks to the upper middle and lower middle positions and preheat the oven to 350°F. Line two rimmed baking sheets with silicone baking mats or parchment paper.

2 In a medium-size bowl, whisk together the flour, salt, baking powder, and baking soda.

3 With an electric mixer on medium-high speed (use the paddle attachment if using a stand mixer), beat together in a large bowl the butter, brown sugar, and granulated sugar until pale and fluffy, 3 to 5 minutes, scraping down the sides and bottom of the bowl with a rubber spatula as needed.

4 Add the eggs one at a time, beating well after each addition. Beat in the vanilla.

5 Reduce the mixer speed to low. Working in batches, add the flour mixture to the creamed sugar mixture. Once again, scrape the sides and bottom of the bowl.

6 With a rubber spatula, fold in the chocolate chips and pecans (never use a mixer on them or it will bash up your perfect chips).

350 grams (2⅔ cups) all-purpose flour

1 teaspoon salt

½ teaspoon baking powder

½ teaspoon baking soda

1 cup (2 sticks, 8 ounces) unsalted butter, cut into 16 pieces, at room temperature

200 grams (1⅛ cups) packed dark brown sugar

100 grams (½ cup) granulated sugar

2 large eggs, at room temperature

2½ teaspoons pure vanilla extract

1 (12-ounce) bag semisweet chocolate chips

½ cup pecans, chopped

7 Scoop about 2 tablespoonfuls of dough onto the prepared baking sheets, spacing them about 2 inches apart. Bake them for 8 to 10 minutes, or until the edges are nicely browned, rotating the position of the baking sheets halfway through baking.

8 Transfer the baking sheets to cooling racks and let cool for 5 minutes, then use a metal spatula to transfer the cookies directly to the racks. Let cool completely and enjoy.

9 Cookies will keep for up to 1 week at room temperature in an airtight container.

Chocolate–Chocolate Chip Cookies
with Salted Caramel Drizzle

I love cookies as much as the next guy, but the star
of the show here is the salted caramel sauce. I make a jar of this and put it on
everything from ice cream to my Cheater Doughnuts (page 236).
I have no doubt you will find endless things to put it on as well, or do as my wife
does and eat it by the spoonful.

1 Adjust two oven racks to the upper middle and lower middle positions and preheat the oven to 350°F. Line two rimmed baking sheets with silicone baking mats or parchment paper.

2 In a medium-size bowl, whisk together the flour, cocoa powder, salt, baking powder, and baking soda.

3 With an electric mixer (use the paddle attachment if using a stand mixer) on medium-high speed, beat together in a large bowl the butter, brown sugar, and granulated sugar until pale and fluffy, 3 to 5 minutes, scraping down the sides and bottom of the bowl with a rubber spatula as needed.

4 Add the eggs one at a time, beating well after each addition. Beat in the vanilla.

5 Reduce the mixer speed to low. Working in batches, add the flour mixture to the creamed sugar mixture. Once again, scrape the sides and bottom of the bowl.

6 With a rubber spatula, fold in the chocolate chips and walnuts (never use a mixer on them or it will bash up your perfect chips).

275 grams (2 cups plus 1 tablespoon) all-purpose flour

75 grams (1 cup plus 1 teaspoon) natural unsweetened cocoa powder

1 teaspoon salt

½ teaspoon baking powder

½ teaspoon baking soda

1 cup (2 sticks, 8 ounces) unsalted butter, cut into 16 pieces, at room temperature

200 grams (1⅛ cups) packed dark brown sugar

100 grams (½ cup) granulated sugar

2 large eggs, at room temperature

1 teaspoon pure vanilla extract

340 grams (1½ cups) bittersweet chocolate chips

½ cup walnuts, chopped

Salted Caramel Sauce (recipe follows)

7   Scoop about 2 tablespoonfuls of dough onto the prepared baking sheets, spacing them about 2 inches apart. Bake them for 8 to 10 minutes, or until the edges are nicely browned, rotating the position of the baking sheets halfway through baking.

8   Transfer the baking sheets to cooling racks and let cool for 5 minutes, then use a metal spatula to transfer the cookies directly to the racks. Let cool completely.

9   Place the cookies on a rimmed baking sheet and drizzle them with the salted caramel sauce.

Salted Caramel Sauce

YIELD: ABOUT 1½ CUPS SAUCE

1 cup granulated sugar
2 tablespoons light corn syrup
¼ cup water
1 cup heavy cream
½ vanilla bean, split, seeds scraped out
¼ cup Greek yogurt
1 teaspoon fleur de sel

1   Stir the sugar, corn syrup, and water in a medium-size saucepan with high sides over high heat until the sugar is completely dissolved. Allow to boil, occasionally swirling the pan but never stirring it. To prevent the sugar crystals from burning, brush the inside of the saucepan with a wet pastry brush. Cook until the mixture becomes dark amber in color, 6 to 8 minutes, or until it registers 350°F on a candy thermometer.

2   While the syrup is cooking, heat the cream and the vanilla bean pod and seeds in a small saucepan over medium heat, until just below a simmer (do not allow it to boil over).

3   Once the sugar comes to temperature, turn off the heat, remove the vanilla bean pod from the cream, and gently pour the cream into the sugar mixture. It will bubble and sputter like crazy; allow it to do so for a few seconds. Turn the heat back on to medium and stir with a heatproof spatula or wooden spoon until the mixture is smooth. Remove from the heat and whisk in the yogurt and fleur de sel until completely emulsified.

4   Use the sauce immediately or store it in an airtight container for up to 1 week at room temperature, although it probably won't last that long!

Aztec
Drinking Chocolate

It may be cold outside, but don't let that ruin your day. Warm your hands and your soul by cradling a mug of this spicy hot chocolate. It's aromatic, rich, and guaranteed to set you right.

2 cups almond milk or whole milk

½ teaspoon cayenne pepper

1 (2 to 3-inch) cinnamon stick

½ vanilla bean, split in half length-wise

Pinch of salt

2½ ounces bittersweet or Mexican chocolate, chopped

Freshly grated nutmeg

1 In a small saucepan over low heat, bring the milk, cayenne, cinnamon, vanilla bean, and salt to a gentle simmer. Simmer for 2 minutes.

2 Add chocolate and gently whisk until completely melted. Turn off the heat and let the flavors meld for about 10 minutes.

3 Strain the drink through a fine-mesh sieve into a clean saucepan and discard the solids. Return to a gentle simmer over low heat. Pour the chocolate into mugs and top with a grating of nutmeg.

I prefer Mexican chocolate over regular chocolate here because of the rich spice profile it adds to the finished product. It can be found in most markets and is ubiquitous in Mexican grocery stores.

Chocolate Cupcakes
with Chocolate Fudge Icing

YIELD: 1 DOZEN CUPCAKES

This is the first cupcake I learned to bake with my grandma and this is also probably my earliest memory of chocolate. I altered this recipe very little from the original cake my grandma made during her career. I did my best to codify the cryptic recipes she jotted down onto many well-seasoned index cards.

For the cupcakes:

1 Adjust an oven rack to the middle position and preheat the oven to 350°F. Place 12 cupcake liners inside a standard 12-cup muffin tin. Lightly coat the liners with baking spray.

2 Place the cocoa powder in a medium-size bowl. Slowly whisk in the boiling water until the mixture is smooth.

3 Sift together the flour, baking soda, powder, and salt.

4 With an electric mixer on medium-high speed (use the paddle attachment if using a stand mixer), beat together in a large bowl the butter and sugar until pale and fluffy, 3 to 5 minutes, scraping down the sides and bottom of the bowl with a rubber spatula as needed.

5 Add the eggs one at a time, beating well after each addition. Beat in the vanilla.

6 Reduce the mixer speed to low. Add the flour in three batches, alternating with the cocoa mixture, scraping down the sides and bottom of bowl between additions.

7 Pour the batter into the prepared muffin cups, filling each about three-quarters full. Bake for 20 to 22 minutes, or until a toothpick inserted into the center of a cupcake comes out clean.

8 Set the muffin tin on a cooling rack and let cool for 10 minutes. Transfer the cupcakes directly to the rack and cool completely.

CUPCAKES:

Baking spray

1½ cups natural unsweetened cocoa powder

2 cups boiling water

2¾ cups cake flour

2 teaspoons baking soda

¾ teaspoon baking powder

½ teaspoon salt

1 cup (2 sticks, 8 ounces) unsalted butter, cut into 16 pieces, at room temperature

2½ cups granulated sugar

4 large eggs, at room temperature

1½ teaspoons pure vanilla extract

ICING:

**½ cup (1 stick, 4 ounces)
unsalted butter, cut into 8
pieces, at room temperature**

**½ cup natural unsweetened
cocoa powder**

½ cup milk

1 teaspoon pure vanilla extract

3½ cups confectioners' sugar

½ teaspoon salt

For the icing:

1 Fill a large bowl with ice and
water (the bowl should only be
half-full).

2 Melt the butter in a 4-quart
saucepan. Whisk in the cocoa
powder until smooth. Slowly
whisk in the milk and vanilla
until smooth, remove from the
heat, and whisk in the sugar and
salt until smooth. Scrape the
mixture into a heatproof bowl
that will fit inside the prepared
ice bath bowl.

3 Set the fudge bowl in the ice
bath and stir until the mixture is
thick enough to spread. Ice the
cupcakes and enjoy.

4 You can prepare the cupcakes
and icing 1 day in advance.
Store the cupcakes and icing in
separate airtight containers at
room temperature until ready to
serve.

Cheater Doughnuts
with Lavender Glaze

YIELD: ABOUT A DOZEN DOUGHNUTS PLUS THE HOLES

Freshly frying up a batch of these doughnuts is one of my absolute favorite ways to spoil my guests. Without all the kneading, waiting, rolling, and so on, this is an easy treat for a host to put together at the last minute, and also makes a great group activity—it won't be hard to find recruits to get in on the punching, frying, and glazing action.

1 Set a wire rack inside a rimmed baking sheet.

2 Fill a Dutch oven, large cast-iron skillet, or other large, heavy-bottomed skillet with high sides with enough oil to reach ½ inch up the sides. Heat the oil over medium-high heat until it registers 350°F on a candy or deep-fat thermometer.

3 Whisk together the almond milk, confectioners' sugar, and lavender buds in a small saucepan. Bring the mixture to a boil over medium-high heat, whisking constantly. Remove the saucepan from the heat and steep the glaze for 10 minutes.

4 Strain the glaze through a fine-mesh sieve into a large bowl.

5 Open the biscuit tins and separate the pieces of dough. Using a 1-inch cutter, punch out the middle of each round of dough. If you don't have a cutter, you can use a plastic bottle cap or an apple corer.

6 Line a plate with three sheets of paper towels. Working in batches, fry the doughnuts and holes until golden brown on both sides, 2 to 3 minutes per side. Chopsticks are great for turning the doughnuts!

7 Drain the doughnuts on the paper towels. Dip them in the glaze and set them on the prepared wire rack to drip dry. Serve immediately.

Vegetable oil
⅓ cup almond milk
1 cup confectioners' sugar, sifted
1 tablespoon culinary-grade lavender buds
2 tubes nonhydrogenated biscuit rolls

If you don't have an oil thermometer, use one of the doughnut holes as a test. If it sinks, the oil isn't hot enough; if it browns too quickly, lower the heat and wait for the oil to cool down a bit.

In the fall I make these into pumpkin spice doughnuts that remind me of the cider mills I went to as a kid in Michigan. Just mix 2 tablespoons of Pumpkin Spice Mix (page 165) for every cup of sugar and whisk together.

Sweet Cheese Blintzes

YIELD: 10 BLINTZES

This recipe is a result of a dear Jewish friend who has celiac disease and had pretty much given up on blintzes altogether. After a little tinkering and a combo of gluten-free starches, I came up with a Paleo/grain-free crêpe recipe that has a multitude of uses. The filling has just the right amount of natural sweetness and a nice fresh zing of lemon.

FILLING:
- ½ cup mascarpone cheese
- ½ cup ricotta cheese
- 1 tablespoon honey
- ½ teaspoon pure vanilla extract
- 1 teaspoon finely grated lemon zest

FOR ASSEMBLY:
- 10 Paleo Crêpes (page 35)
- Grass-fed butter or coconut oil
- Your desired jam

For the filling: Using a spatula, work the filling ingredients together until they are well mixed.

To assemble:

1 Lay a crêpe flat and spoon 2 generous tablespoons of the filling into the middle. Fold in the sides, and starting at the bottom, roll up to enclose the filling. Heat 1 tablespoon of butter in a medium-size skillet over medium-high heat until bubbling and fry each blintz, seam side down, until slightly crispy and warmed throughout.

2 Top with your desired jam.

Top these with the One-Step Apricot Jam (page 29) or Three-Ingredient Blackberry Jam (page 28).

Seasonal Streusel

YIELD: 4 TO 6 SERVINGS

FOR THE TOPPING

- 1½ cups packed light brown sugar
- 1 cup all-purpose flour
- ½ cup old-fashioned rolled oats
- 4 ounces (1 stick) unsalted butter, chilled and cut into small pieces
- 1 teaspoon ground cinnamon
- ½ teaspoon salt

FOR THE FILLING

- 6 cups fresh fruit, cut into bite-sized pieces
- ½ cup granulated sugar
- 2 tablespoons cornstarch
- 1 (½-inch) piece ginger, finely grated (1 teaspoon)
- 2 teaspoons fresh lemon juice

For the topping: For the crispiest topping, combine the sugar, flour, oats, butter, cinnamon, and salt in a food processor and pulse until the mixture resembles wet sand. Otherwise, whisk together the sugar, flour, oats, cinnamon, and salt in a large bowl. Then, using your hands, work the butter into the mixture until everything is fully incorporated.

For the filling:

1. Adjust an oven rack to the middle position and preheat the oven to 375°F.

2. In a large bowl, toss the fruit, sugar, cornstarch, ginger (if using), and lemon juice together until thoroughly combined. Transfer the filling to an 8 x 8-inch baking dish or to another oven-safe vessel of similar capacity.

3. Top the fruit with the crumble. Bake until bubbly and nice and firm on top, 30 to 35 minutes. Transfer the dish to a cooling rack and allow to cool about 15 minutes before serving.

In the summer months I use a combo of strawberries, blueberries, and peaches. In the fall I love my apples and pears, so I add ½ teaspoon ground allspice to the mix.

Bubbles and Peaches

YIELD: 4 SERVINGS

Peaches are always my indication that summer is finally here to stay.
I like to buy a big batch, wash them and remove the stones, freeze half for
smoothies, and use the other half for cooking right away. There
are so many varieties to choose from, but the best to use in this recipe are
referred to as freestone. This means the flesh will come away from
the stone easily when cut, making it easy for you to achieve nice beautiful
wedges of fruit. The more stubborn clingstone peaches
are better for jams and preserving.

1 In a small saucepan, combine the sugar, sparkling wine, water, and vanilla bean pod and seeds. Bring to a simmer over medium heat and cook, stirring, just until the sugar dissolves. Be mindful not to simmer for too long or the bubbles will dissipate.

2 Place the peaches in a large, heatproof bowl. Pour the syrup over the peaches, cover with plastic wrap, and infuse for at least 30 minutes.

3 Top with freshly torn mint leaves and a dollop of labne. Enjoy warm or cold with a pinch of the mint over ice cream.

1 cup granulated sugar
1 cup sparkling white wine, such as champagne or cava
1 cup water
½ vanilla bean, split lengthwise, seeds scraped out
4 peaches, pitted and cut into wedges to make 3 cups (frozen will work in a pinch)
5 fresh mint leaves, very finely sliced
Dollop of labne (optional)

Cava is my go-to for cheap bubbles. Trust me,
your friends will be none the wiser.
After scraping the vanilla bean seeds and paste out of the
pod, rub it with the sugar between your fingers to coax the
maximum amount of vanilla flavor from the bean.

Lemon Chamomile
Sorbet

YIELD: ABOUT 3 CUPS SORBET

If you don't happen to have an ice cream maker, pour the liquid into a freezer-safe container and freeze, scrape down the mixture, and break it up every so often to make a refreshing granita.

2 sachets chamomile tea (preferably Mariage Frères)
2 cups water
1½ cups granulated sugar
1 large egg white
¾ cup freshly squeezed lemon juice (from 4 to 5 organic lemons)

1 Combine the tea sachets and water in a microwave-safe container and microwave for 2½ minutes on HIGH.

2 Let the tea infuse on the counter for another 2 minutes.

3 Remove the sachets and place the tea water and sugar in a small saucepan over medium heat. Stir until all the sugar has dissolved.

4 Meanwhile, in the mixing bowl of a stand mixer fitted with the whisk attachment, beat the egg white on medium-high speed until soft peaks form.

5 With the machine running, slowly pour the hot sugar mixture down the side of the bowl.

6 Add the lemon juice, cover, and chill in the fridge until completely cold.

7 For sorbet, freeze in ice cream maker according to the manufacturer's instructions. If you want to make a granite, freeze in a Pyrex or other suitable container, making sure to scrape it about every 30 minutes or so, until chunky and icy.

Rhubarb
Popsicles

This recipe happened completely by accident. I was originally intending to create a spring cocktail and ended up freezing the base—and voilà, a Popsicle was born. I then took it a step further and added the ginger beer for a nice, spicy-sweet kick.

1 In medium-size bowl or large liquid measuring cup, gently stir the syrup and ginger beer together. Pour into Popsicle molds and follow package instructions for inserting Popsicle sticks.

2 Freeze for 8 hours, or until solid.

3 Run the molds under hot water for a few seconds to help release the pops.

1 cup Rhubarb Strawberry Simple Syrup (recipe follows)

12 ounces ginger beer or sparkling water

Rhubarb Strawberry Simple Syrup

1 Combine the sugar and water in a medium-size saucepan. Bring to a boil over medium-high heat, stirring until the sugar is completely dissolved. Add the rhubarb and strawberries, lower the heat to medium, and simmer for 12 to 15 minutes, or until they're completely softened.

2 Remove the saucepan from the heat, cover tightly with foil, and allow to steep for at least 2 hours. Strain through a fine-mesh strainer into a glass jar or container. Use immediately or store in an airtight container for up to 1 week in the fridge.

2 cups granulated sugar

2 cups water

6 to 8 rhubarb stalks, sliced (4 cups)

3 cups strawberries, hulled and quartered (2½ cups)

Save that reserved pulp after you strain the syrup. It's a delicious match to whisk into your morning yogurt or as a topping for the Sweet Cheese Blintzes (page 239).
If you want to substitute agave nectar, reduce the sweetener amount to 1½ cups of agave. My rule of thumb is ¼ cup less per cup, since agave is more concentrated. You can experiment with other sugars but it will alter the color slightly.

This recipe works well with the Lemongrass and Kaffir Lime Simple Syrups on page 191.

Strawberry Sorbet

YIELD: 4 TO 6 SERVINGS

Want strawberry sorbet without the wait?
The strawberries from my smoothies do double duty here and will have you
enjoying a fresh-from-scratch dessert in less than five minutes.

1 Let the frozen strawberries stand at room temperature for about 10 minutes, to soften slightly.

2 Place the frozen strawberries in a food processor and process until they resemble wet sand.

3 With the machine running, slowly stream in the syrup and continue to process until the mixture becomes completely smooth.

4 Wrap the shortbread cookies in a kitchen towel, twisting the towel so they stay contained, and give them a few good whacks against the counter to pulverize them into crumbs.

5 Place a tablespoon of the crumbs in a small bowl or plate and top with a scoop of the sorbet and a drizzle of the balsamic glaze.

1 (16-ounce bag) frozen strawberries
⅓ cup Basil Lime Simple Syrup (page 188)
4 shortbread cookies
Balsamic Glaze (page 133)

When stored in the freezer, this sorbet becomes very hard,
so be sure to soften it in the microwave, using 10-second
blasts until it's soft enough to scoop.

Cherry Clafoutis Cookies

YIELD: ABOUT 24 COOKIES

I really hate wasting ingredients, so I came up with this cookie recipe when I was looking for something to do with all the leftover pulp from making almond milk. Set your oven to 200 degrees, spread out the almond pulp in a thin even layer, and let it dry out for about two hours. If it clumps in large pieces, give it a few pulses in the food processor to make a nice fine powder. These cookies are more like little shortbreads and won't spread like traditional drop cookies.

2 cups almond flour (from the dried pulp, or else from recipe on page 33)
4 tablespoons unsalted butter, softened
¼ cup honey
½ teaspoon pure vanilla extract
¼ teaspoon salt
½ cup dried cherries, chopped

1. Adjust two oven racks to the upper middle and lower middle positions and preheat the oven to 350°F. Line two rimmed baking sheets with a silicone baking mats or parchment paper.

2. Combine the almond flour, butter, honey, vanilla, and salt in a large bowl with a rubber spatula. Once a smooth paste has been formed, stir in the cherries.

3. Spread a piece of plastic wrap on a work surface. Transfer the dough to the plastic and shape it into a log about 12 inches long. Wrap the dough in the plastic and gently roll it to smooth out the log.

4. Freeze the dough for 30 minutes, or until firm. Unwrap the dough and place it on a cutting board. Using a sharp knife, cut it into ½-inch-thick rounds.

5. Arrange the dough rounds on the prepared baking sheets, spacing them about 2 inches apart. Bake them for 10 to 12 minutes, or until the edges are nicely browned, rotating the position of the baking sheets halfway through baking.

6. Transfer the baking sheets to cooling racks and let cool for 5 minutes, then use a metal spatula to transfer the cookies directly to the racks. Let cool completely and enjoy.

7. The cookies will keep in an airtight container for up to 1 week at room temperature.

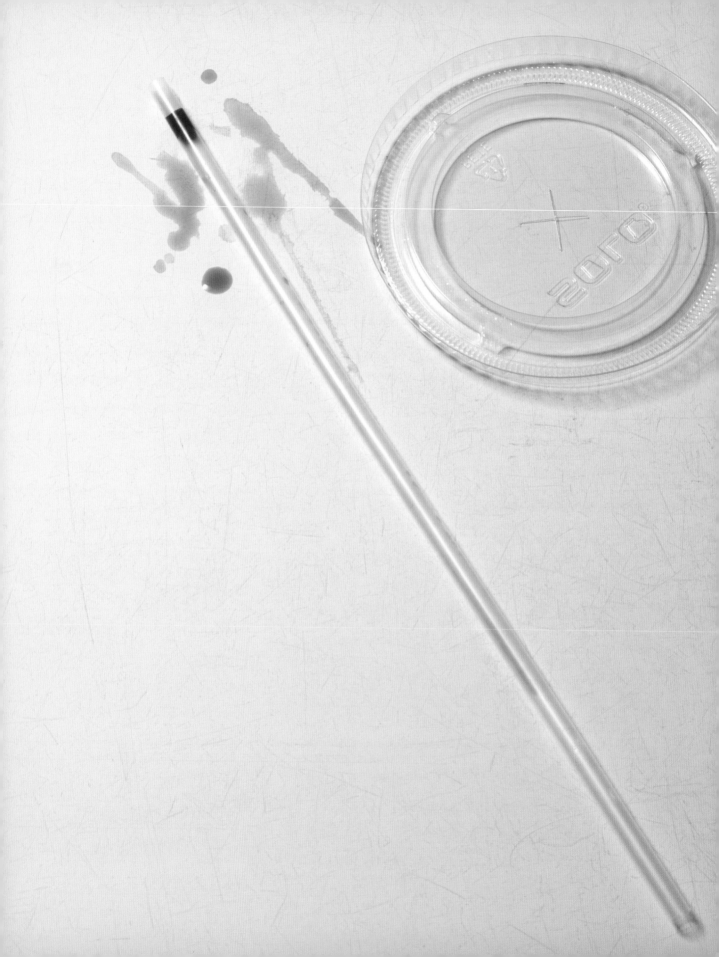

Index